ELITISM

PROVOCATIONS

ELITISM
A PROGRESSIVE DEFENCE

ELIANE GLASER

SERIES EDITOR:
YASMIN ALIBHAI-BROWN

Biteback Publishing

First published in Great Britain in 2020 by
Biteback Publishing Ltd, London
Copyright © Eliane Glaser 2020

ISBN 978-1-78590-607-7

10 9 8 7 6 5 4 3 2 1

A CIP catalogue record for this book is available from the British Library.

Set in Stempel Garamond

Printed and bound in Great Britain by
CPI Group (UK) Ltd, Croydon CR0 4YY

MIX
Paper from
responsible sources
FSC
www.fsc.org   FSC® C020471

Contents

Introduction

I'LL SAY IT up front: I am a member of the liberal, metropolitan elite. I live in north London, I work in the media, I'm a writer and – God forbid – I teach at a university. I don't actually feel very elite, riding around on a second-hand bicycle, a member of the journalistic precariat, on a shoestring lectureship. Don't get me wrong: I live a very comfortable life. But something peculiar has happened over the past few years. Never mind that eight people, all men, now own as much wealth as half the world's population. Never mind that CEOs earn 300 times the salary of the average worker. From newspaper commentary, intelligent magazines, TV talk shows, radio phone-ins and social media comes the same message, loud and clear: that it is people like me who are now the masters of the universe.

Experts, professionals and those who work in the arts, publishing, culture or the media have become public enemy number one.

Those in the firing line know this is happening. They whisper about it in workplace corridors, or in the privacy of their own homes. But they daren't say it in public. Why? Because compared to the more serious losers in all this, the gig-economy bikers for Deliveroo or Uber, care workers paid less than the minimum wage, or shelf-stackers on zero-hours contracts, they are doing all right. But this is a trap. Playing off those on the lowest incomes against the overstretched intelligentsia has paid off brilliantly for the burgeoning financial and managerial classes.

This book puts its head above the parapet to call this outrage out. It is an alibi book for all those doing their best and slogging away to keep us safe, to fight for our rights, to question assumptions and to create brilliant and beautiful works of art. This book is not only for doctors, lawyers, scientists, thinkers, publishers, journalists and artists of every variety, but for all those who appreciate what they do. Which is an awful lot of people.

The coronavirus crisis has shown us how much we rely not only on those who save our lives but also on those who make life worth living.

Anti-elitism is a familiar truism to anyone tuned in to media and public discussion over the past five years. Phrases like 'liberal elite' are bandied about in press commentary without us really knowing what they mean – or if they even refer to anything real. They are bogey words that prevent us from diagnosing and therefore strategising an escape from our political and cultural quagmire. The constant reiteration just amplifies rather than analyses the problem.

This book will take a step back and attempt to cut through the endless, self-referential commentary by placing it in vital historical perspective. I'll show why our embattled elites should be not embarrassed but proud – and angry. The real economic elites have pulled off a grand deceit. They are diverting public anger away from the obscene profiteering of billionaires, banks and global corporations and turning it onto cultural and educational high standards.

As I will argue, the populist right and the powerful

interests they serve are deploying cultural populism as their primary strategy; but what is less often remarked upon is that this is being enabled by a terrified left, quixotically pursuing the wrong solutions. Progressives are letting the real economic elites get away with it – in fact, they are aiding and abetting them – by accepting the false frames of the culture wars. Cultural and educational organisations, and the agencies that fund them, are prioritising a modish agenda of 'democratisation', outreach and user engagement, and the resulting emphasis on symbolic representation functions as a proxy for real structural and economic equality. Liberals no longer have the confidence to advocate for excellence and legitimate critical and political authority: the 'liberal elite' slur is just as common in broadsheet commentary and left-of-centre political speeches as it is on far-right social media. It is true that in many cases, wealth and social privilege does correlate with political office, higher education and cultural production and consumption. But as I will show, it doesn't have to be that way.

This surrender to cultural populism is resulting in the concentration of power and wealth at the top of the social hierarchy and a race to the bottom when it comes to artistic and educational quality: a society starkly divided economically with a culture that is increasingly undistinguished and undifferentiated. Culture and expression are being levelled; power and money are not. While the real elites are let off the hook, our arts and education are diminished, becoming bland and apologetic. When we have destroyed all sources of reputable knowledge we will call that equality, while real inequality remains conveniently out of the picture. Vast disparities of wealth and power thus escape scrutiny, while everything that gives life value and meaning has to fight for its very existence.

The anti-elitism that we see everywhere around us is presented as a new development, as ordinary people finally having their say, but it is in fact part of a long anti-intellectual tradition stretching back through Nazi Germany to nineteenth-century America. In the course of this short book I'll pick apart our society's kneejerk confounding of education and culture on one hand and social and economic privilege on the other. Only by doing so can we start to defend good elitism. We have given up attempting to define what constitutes truth and beauty, dismissing both as necessarily posh. Yet from the eighteenth century onwards, a series of thinkers and writers set out to do precisely that.

I will point to another largely forgotten historical tradition, running through the writings of William Morris and nineteenth-century workers' education initiatives, and on into twentieth-century avant-garde art, media and architecture. This alternative tradition envisaged the most challenging ideas and the highest culture as fully legible to the least prosperous people. By reviving its principles, we can begin to imagine a fairer future in both senses of the word: a future society that values both equality and aesthetics. It's time for a progressive defence of elitism.

One

The New Anti-Elitism

As AN ADJECTIVE, the word 'elite' still has a positive meaning: as in elite athlete, or elite travel agency. As a noun, it's now wholly negative. Home Secretary Priti Patel has laid in to the 'north London metropolitan, liberal elite'. The *Mail on Sunday* hailed Boris Johnson's election victory as a triumph over 'vain, secluded elites of London', lambasting what it called the 'Corbyn-supporting, Boris-hating metropolitans' and the 'left-liberal upper deck'. Johnson's triumph meant the arrival of 'the real Britain': 'normal people living in normal places and dealing with all the hard-edged problems of real life'; people who are 'sick and tired' of the 'political class' and the BBC, 'the megaphone of the liberal elite'. Dominic

Cummings advertised his disdain for 'Oxbridge English graduates who chat about Lacan at dinner parties with TV producers'. 'Blame Rich, Overeducated Elites as Society Frays' ran a Bloomberg headline. Australia's *Daily Telegraph* bemoaned what it called former Liberal Prime Minister Malcolm Turnbull's 'elitist attitude' and the growing gulf between the 'working class' and the 'talking class'.

A lot of this is, of course, bound up with Brexit, which is often now referred to as if it were a prime cause – of public anger, bitter political division and many ills besides. But Brexit is a symptom of a broader political trend, with roots that stretch further back in time. And it has also served as a dredged-out channel through which this growing trend has gushed. For *The Sun*'s Rod Liddle, it represented 'a revolt against a ruling liberal political class which has caused untold havoc at home and mayhem and murder abroad'. The *Mail*'s Quentin Letts saw it as 'a massive custard pie smack in the face' for 'our dominating elite of parliamentarians, lobbyists, bankers, artists, political theorists, clergy, academics and sterile aesthetes'. The *Mail* denounced judges as the 'enemies of the people', and Michael Gove declared that 'Britain has had enough of experts'.

Those who voted Remain, it is routinely assumed, are members of 'the elite'. Dominic Cummings refers to 'educated Remainer campaigner types', the head of JD Wetherspoon, a prominent Brexit supporter, attacked 'elite Remainers', and the trope has been repeated by the *Telegraph*, the *Express* and Spiked. Brexit has helped to erode rationality and truth in four ways: by disparaging experts as unforgivably pompous, by questioning their worth (they didn't see this coming), by deprivileging economic facts (this is about national pride, not GDP), and by undermining the principle of reasoned debate through the delegitimising of one side. How can Remainers be powerful when they are not supposed to now exist?

As with Brexit, so with Trump. 'The experts are terrible!' he told his fans. Trump has – famously – been employing the chilling phrase 'enemies of the people' to describe broadcasters and newspapers he doesn't like. Even using the phrase 'the people' is, of course, a way of implicitly attacking elites. The same goes for the oft-repeated policy priority of investing in Britain's 'towns' – it has the ring of long-overdue redistribution, but it also carries a nasty undertone of anti-cosmopolitanism.

In this book, I do not intend to add yet another voice to the worthwhile, yet somewhat tiresome, chorus of demagogue-bashing. In order to redress the gross injustices in our society we need to challenge not just wealth and power but the public licence that legitimates it. Anti-elitism is that licence. Progressives might feel like they're socking it to Trump, Farage, Johnson and the rest in their verbal campaigns, but as long as they continue to tacitly accept anti-elitism as the new political front line, their opposition will be toothless. The philistine oligopoly would like nothing more than for those who believe in liberal democracy to conclude ruefully that, yes, they are stuck in their bubbles and perhaps they do therefore have it coming. Public anger is thereby successfully deflected away from financial and corporate power and onto those who work to improve society, increase the sum of human knowledge and hold our leaders to account.

Not only does the targeting of a relatively vulnerable intelligentsia facilitate unchecked power, therefore; it also contributes to the erosion of knowledge itself. 'I honestly don't think this "fact-checking" business … is anything more than … one more out of touch, elitist media-type thing,' said author and Republican strategist Jeffrey Lord (estimated net worth: $5 million). The tagging of accuracy as inherently upper crust is key to this devaluation of knowledge. Fake news has become a journalistic cliché, the subject of a great deal of columnist hand-wringing. Yet defending truth is now like lifting up a table while standing on it, because as a society we have collectively accepted the pairing of veracity and elites.

Thus climate science, and therefore efforts to combat global heating, are also undermined because they are 'elite'. 'How on earth can the elite lecture us about climate change?' demands the *Express*. 'Climate elitists wage war on regular people' ran a headline in the *Toronto Sun*. In early 2020, while bushfires raged across Australia, the politician and climate sceptic Craig Kelly denied the link between the fires and the global temperature rise. He was interviewed on BBC Radio 4's *Today* programme by Nick Robinson along with Catherine King, a Labor politician; when she expressed dismay at Kelly's position, Robinson countered that Kelly's party had won an election by representing the views of the people. King sighed with frustration at this now dominant line of questioning.

There is a chink in truth's armour, and it is growing into a great gaping gulf: it is the idea that what the public believes and says must be taken at face value, even if they are wrong, their views are destroying the planet and they are patently being misinformed by vested interests. Top-down manipulation of public opinion – how 1970s! You can't possibly be dusting off that old Marxist notion of 'false consciousness' – that citizens are persuaded to vote against their own economic interests by well-resourced politicians via a compliant media; that would be unconscionably patronising. Such arguments usually prompt the response: 'People aren't stupid.' But as the science journalist David Robson points out in *The Intelligence Trap*, numerous studies have shown that we are all duped: IQ has nothing to do with it.

We may be familiar with the anti-elitism coming from the far right – from Stephen Yaxley-Lennon aka Tommy Robinson, Paul Staines aka Guido Fawkes, and Steve Bannon, who has complained that 'elites have taken all the upside for themselves and pushed the downside to the working- and middle-class Americans'. Far-right conspiracy theorists on the dark web conjure the spectre of 'The Illuminati' – a cabal of powerful intellectuals pulling the strings of both culture and finance.

What is less often discussed is the fact that this framing is reinforced by those who are themselves labelled the 'liberal elite'. Jeremy Corbyn repeatedly referred to 'the establishment elite'. The Labour MP Stephen Kinnock – himself the son of an ex-Labour leader and the husband of the former Prime Minister of Denmark – distanced himself from the 'metropolitan elite'. Another Labour MP, Rebecca Long-Bailey, vowed to 'wage war on the political establishment'. The *Guardian* columnist Jonathan Freedland wrote that the two main parties' handling of Brexit represents 'an indictment of our entire political class'. The death of liberal democracy, liberals self-diagnose, has been hastened by the failures and smug arrogance of... liberal democracy; and its demise is hastened yet further.

This populist conception of the people versus a metropolitan elite or political establishment is highly damaging. And commentators refer to this cultural split as if describing the weather, or observing a phenomenon that has bubbled right up from the authentic left-behind heartlands of the post-industrial north. These populists draw on wellsprings of poverty, disenfranchisement and discontent that are real. But shifting the fault line to people versus elites is not organic but the artificial product of top-down ideological re-engineering. Yaxley-Lennon has worked as a 'correspondent' for The Rebel Media, the website run by Canadian conservative polemicist and conspiracy theorist Ezra Levant and financed by wealthy donors who include Robert Shillman, the head of a multi-billion-pound US technology firm. Shillman is just one of many right-wing populist financiers – from Robert Mercer to the Koch brothers – bankrolling and orchestrating the shift from economic to cultural division around the world.

Anti-elitism lumps together two different constituencies that are generally diametrically opposed: wealthy financiers and corporate executives on one hand and liberal politicians, professionals and media commentators on the other. On Fox News, for example, the arch-right-wing radical Steve Hilton has laid into 'the elitists in finance, big business, the media and politics'. This is a brilliant and devastating coup, since it allows public anger at the one to be simultaneously directed at the other.

The populist right have also created a false equivalence between the left and power. Even just being left-wing, or speaking up for society's victims, has acquired the taint of elitism: after the rapper Stormzy criticised the government over its response to the Grenfell fire, Brendan O'Neill branded him 'fully part of the cultural elite'. The phrase 'liberal elite' has gained huge traction: it has acquired the ring of truth, even among the supposedly progressive commentariat. Yet in the UK, it's the Conservative Party that's been dominant for the nineteenth, twentieth and so far the twenty-first centuries. Corbyn took Labour to the left, but failed to win office. In the US, aside from the rather centrist Obama, Republicans have taken over politics at both state and federal level.

In 1989, Francis Fukuyama famously declared that the great ideological battles between left and right, East and West were over and that Western liberal democracy had won. He was wrong, but not in the way that people usually think. Rather than Fukuyama's centre-right capitalist liberal democracy, it's actually progressive politics that has swept the board – at least on the level of language. The right used to defend the rich's right to keep their cash, and to claim that inequality was justified by hard graft. But now they purport to be the true friends of ordinary working families, the blue-collar left-behind, the just-about-managing. The right's theft of progressive ideas reveals just how far those ideas have triumphed – but in terms of *power*, the progressives have lost. Nonetheless, alt-right polemicists have been able to cement the lie that it's liberals who are now running the show. Alt-right and 'alt-light' social media personalities and commentators – foremost among them Jordan Peterson – accord a ludicrous degree of power and influence to rapidly shrinking humanities departments in ailing universities. They claim that political correctness is an oppressive force, constraining the put-upon 'mainstream'.

The creation of the myth of an elite left has been accomplished to a large extent by exploiting the slipperiness of the term 'liberal'. The right use it to refer to the left. But the hard left use it too. Young radicals lob the insult 'boomer liberalism' at those they regard as complacent, centrist dads. This insult has proved very useful for the right: it helps them present the whole of the left, not just the moderate, centrist bit, as secure and dominant.

Another resonance of the word 'liberal' has been employed by the populist right to reinforce an illusory alliance between progressive politics and global capitalism. 'Liberalism' – such an unhelpfully weasel word – can mean both left-of-centre ideals and also financial liberalism, the freedom of capital to run friction-free rings around the world. This is great news for those hellbent on rerouting the hostility that should be aimed at banks and multinationals onto a fictional bloated leftist establishment. In 2016, Breitbart characterised the Davos summit as bringing together '2,500 key leftist politicians, intellectuals, journalists, and a slew of multinational corporate cronies to discuss shaping global, regional, and industrial agendas to best divide the economic spoils'. In a speech the same year, Theresa May declared that 'liberalism and globalisation ... have left too many people behind', melding economic liberalism with the liberal left.

The artificial yoking-together of global financial dominance with cosmopolitan intellectualism is carried out with the help of a handy antisemitic stereotype: the prosperous Wandering Jew. George Soros is a regular bogeyman here – because as well as being Jewish he is one of the few progressive financiers. David Goodhart seemed unperturbed by the nastier resonances of his elevation of native 'Somewheres' over worldly 'Everywheres'. May was criticised for claiming that 'if you're a citizen of the world, you're a citizen of nowhere' in another speech, as it echoed the Nazi framing of Jews as 'rootless cosmopolitans'. Yet although this criticism identified her use of an antisemitic trope, it didn't get at the way the slur is used to undermine not only Jews but also egalitarian politics.

How useful for the populist right that it takes some spadework to turn these terms the right way up again;

to prise apart the false conjunctions and restore the real divisions to their correct, opposing sides of the argument. But we need to do this work if we want to see our ideological labyrinth from above, and begin to plot a way out.

The populist right have turned class struggle into the culture wars, and replaced the fight against economic inequality with anti-intellectualism. We are led to believe that it's not big businesses that are the problem – after all, they are 'wealth creators' and job providers. Instead, we are told, it's lofty standards in education, quality in culture – and big government. Because governments bailed out banks after the crash, the populist right have succeeded in converting what should have been an economic crisis into a political one: the people have turned against the very political 'elites' who are the only ones able to regulate and rein in financial power.

Two

Anti-Elitism Has a History

THOSE WHO CLAIM that the old elites 'have had their day', and that what is necessary is a transfer of 'power to the people', talk as if this 'remedy' had not been advocated by a range of dodgy types at numerous points over the past several centuries. As a glance at Google's Ngram Viewer illustrates, use of the words 'elite', 'political elite' and 'liberal elite' has risen exponentially in recent decades. But anti-elitism is not new. During the Third Reich, Nazis stereotyped Jews as rootless intellectuals. They famously banned avant-garde 'degenerate' art, fired academics en masse and burned books. At one bonfire, propaganda minister Joseph Goebbels declared that 'the era of extreme Jewish intellectualism is now at an end … The future

German man will not just be a man of books, but a man of character.' The Nazi newspaper *Illustrierter Beobachter* published pictures of what it called 'traitors of the people': left-wing politicians, lawyers, journalists, theatre critics, writers and pacifists who'd all had their German citizenship revoked. The antisemitic trope of the rootless cosmopolitan was also deployed by Joseph Stalin in the 1950s to enforce allegiance to the Soviet Union. His targets were Jewish writers, critics, scientists and other thinkers he considered to be associated with 'bourgeois' Western influences.

As we've seen in comments by Theresa May and Priti Patel, this stereotype is echoed today – albeit unwittingly – in references to the 'north London metropolitan elite' and the 'chattering classes'. Lest Conservatives be under the impression that they have made an authentic connection with blue-collar voters based on a genuine alignment of interests, rather than following a cookie-cutter ideological playbook replicated around the world, let's remind ourselves that in Hungary, Viktor Orbán has called his political opponents 'people without a country' and has launched a campaign against George Soros. The same line has been pushed in contemporary Germany, the Netherlands, France, Poland and the Czech Republic. And, of course, in America, where Trump claims that 'globalists' are undermining American interests.

Trump is in fact invoking a long tradition of anti-elitism that stretches back through American history. The Populist movement of the late nineteenth century started out as a genuine collective campaign by hard-pressed farmers against corporate and financial power. Yet what began as a progressive grassroots movement morphed into something darker during the course of the twentieth century. By the 1950s, fascism was on the rise in America, personified by Senator Joseph McCarthy. In his 1963 book *Anti-Intellectualism in American Life*, the historian Richard Hofstadter documented this suspicion of 'the critical mind', manifest also in the 1952 election triumph of Republican Dwight Eisenhower, who was fond of belittling academics, over Democrat Adlai Stevenson, who was renowned for his eloquence and erudition: Richard Nixon labelled him an 'egghead'. Nixon, for his part, attempted to appeal to those he called the 'hard hats', while his Vice-President, Spiro

Agnew, disparaged an 'effete corps of impudent snobs who characterise themselves as intellectuals'. During the 1970s, American neoconservatives developed a theory about a group of powerful people they called the 'new class': university-educated intellectuals radicalised by the countercultural social movements of the 1960s, who were apparently attempting to undermine traditional America. This notion was popularised by economists Milton and Rose Friedman in their bestselling book and TV series *Free to Choose*.

The mid-century conservative commentator William F. Buckley proclaimed, 'I should sooner live in a society governed by the first 2,000 names in the Boston telephone directory than in a society governed by the 2,000 faculty members of Harvard University.' The segregationist Alabama governor George Wallace described his critics as 'pointy-headed college professors'. In 1969, the New York mayoral candidate Mario Procaccino, a conservative Democrat, described his rival, the more progressive John Lindsay, as a 'limousine liberal'. Joseph McCarthy himself, a previously obscure senator, rose to prominence with paranoid accusations that Communists had infiltrated the government: the McCarthyite legacy helps to explain how conservatives feel able to claim – in the face of the evidence – that the left are now politically dominant. The anti-elitism of the McCarthyites fed into the John Birch Society, a right-wing group founded in the Cold War to fight Communism and advocate for small government, and that spirit fuelled in turn the rise of arch-right-wing anti-elitists Pat Buchanan, Rush Limbaugh, Irving Kristol and Bill O'Reilly in the second half of the twentieth century.

Republican Presidents from Eisenhower to Reagan to George W. Bush have all dumbed themselves down and posed as downtrodden outsiders, attacking what they portray as the intellectual and political establishment. Reagan's anti-elitism was directed at government: in a 1964 speech he aligned himself with ordinary Americans against the 'intellectual elite in a far-distant capitol'. Similarly, Bush sided with 'the C students' in a 2001 Yale commencement address. During Bill Clinton's presidency, the social critic Christopher Lasch complained in his influential book *The Revolt of the Elites and the Betrayal of Democracy* that 'upper-middle-class liberals' had turned into 'petulant, self-righteous, intolerant' scolds, looking down on Middle America. In a 2004 attack ad, the right-wing Club for Growth told Democrat Howard Dean to 'take his tax-hiking, government-expanding, latte-drinking, sushi-eating, Volvo-driving, *New York Times*-reading, body-piercing, Hollywood-loving, left-wing freak show back to Vermont, where it belongs'. This trend has continued more recently in the Tea Party, that fake grassroots 'revolt' against Washington 'elites', and of course in the contemporary Trumpian mutation: 'I love the poorly educated!' he told his fans.

Milton Friedman's challenge to 'sell ideas like soap' has been taken up by conservative think tanks including the Cato Institute, the Heritage Foundation, the American Enterprise Institute, the Sarah Scaife Foundation and the Bradley Foundation, and propagated via Republican political strategists from Kevin Phillips and Roger Ailes in the late 1960s to Lee Atwater in the late 1980s, to Steve Bannon today. These thinkers have persuaded swathes of the American electorate that social and cultural values are more important than economics

– and their anger should therefore be redirected towards those liberal elites.

As well as stretching back through American history, this is a template that's followed around the world. Here in the UK, it's promoted by think tanks including Policy Exchange and the Institute of Economic Affairs, and in the media, particularly Rupert Murdoch's press. Murdoch's empire originated in Australia, where anti-elitism is particularly virulent: from the 1980s onwards, conservative think tanks like the Institute of Public Affairs followed the American example and began to turn the public debate away from issues of corporate profiteering, tax avoidance and rent-seeking behaviour and onto cultural and educational divides. The right-wing Australian politician Pauline Hanson wrote *The Truth* in 1997 to mark the launch of her One Nation party; a chapter was devoted to attacking what she called 'cognitive' elites and their 'betrayal' of the real Australia. In 2003, the conservative former Prime Minister Tony Abbott wrote the foreword to a book by legal academic David Flint, *The Twilight of the Elites*; in it, he laid into 'the assumption that characterises so many people in the media, academe and administration that "we" know better than "them"'. Former conservative MPs Mark Latham and Ross Cameron joined forces with the Australian *Spectator*'s right-wing controversialist Rowan Dean for a talk show on the broadcaster Sky. The show was named *Outsiders*, a riposte to 'an out-of-touch, inner-city leftist class'.

The same tropes crop up everywhere from Modi's India to Bolsonaro's Brazil. We may roll our eyes at these wannabe autocrats, but they are legitimated and under-pinned by their underdog reputation – Modi's humble origins as a tea seller and Bolsonaro's resistance to West-ern imperialism. Matteo Salvini purports to be 'speaking for the people' against a 'liberal' elite. And the author Ece Temelkuran reminds us that the kind of anti-elite language that seems new, authentic and empowering of left-behind, ordinary folk in the UK is actually where the current post-democratic dictatorship of Recep Tayyip Erdoğan in her native Turkey began. 'It started fifteen years ago,' she writes, 'with a phenomenon that will now be familiar to you, when intellectuals and journalists reacted to a nascent populism with the self-critical question: "Are we out of touch?" To counter that possibility, they widened the parameters of public debate to include those who were said to be representatives of "real people".' Truth, she writes, was split into two: elite truth and the truth of ordinary people. The truth of ordinary people is authentic, the truth of the elites a lie. Heart is valued over head, emotion over reason. No wonder we're in a post-truth age.

Amidst calls for the old elites to be pushed off their pedestals, and triumphant statements that the old establishment is finally giving way to new voices and new forms of empowerment, it is easy to forget that anti-elitism has a long history. This is exacerbated by the fact that we are arguably in the most amnesiac era there's ever been. This erasure of the past allows us to kid ourselves that we are ushering in a novel era of progressive equality, and to ignore the dark uses to which anti-elitism has been put – in the past, and again now. It's as if *Fahrenheit 451* hadn't been written.

Anti-elitism has a history, therefore, but there is something distinctive and noxious about the contemporary strain. So, what is new about the new anti-elitism? First, our era has seen the industrialisation of message-making by political parties and multinationals: the unprecedented deployment of highly sophisticated PR which has engineered the ideological reversals and inversions I'm describing in this book. Second, progressives and cultural organisations have totally lost their nerve. There was in the past a lively opposition between highbrow and popular culture, between discernment and bums on seats. But now, those former defenders are on the back foot, panicked into adopting commercialised culture because they mistakenly believe it's more authentic and democratic. And third, these attacks on journalism, culture, big ideas and political institutions are coinciding with the advent of digital technology, data, AI and algorithmic determinism, which is eroding wholesale those creaky yet essential bastions of quality, oversight and representation.

In the society of the spectacle, fame is proving more psychologically attractive than fortune. Money can't buy you love, but 'likes' feel like recognition and approval, which it turns out we all crave more than we knew. That is why it's possible for the dispossessed to make common cause with the non-illustrious rich. Both envy newspaper columnists, bestselling novelists and professional film critics. Those northern and coastal towns – Blackpool, Broadstairs and Birmingham – used to be glamorous destinations in their own right. London is not just more affluent than the regions now; it's become culturally much more important. That is what metropolitan and cosmopolitan mean. Culture has become the currency of envy just as it is being cut back and centralised. We all want a piece, but there is less and less to go around.

Three

Elites and 'Elites'

I N THE EARLY years of the twenty-first century, there was a brief effervescence of interest in inequality. Two books helped to shock the yawning commentariat into sitting up. One was *The Spirit Level* by Richard Wilkinson and Kate Pickett, which showed that inequality is bad for everyone, even the rich. The other was *Capital in the Twenty-First Century* by Thomas Piketty, which used hard economics to explain the rise of inequality in the modern world. Think tanks on left and right, from Westminster to Washington, were all cottoning on to the benefits of evening things up for everyone. That moment has now passed.

Low-income voters are everywhere voting for parties whose policies cause them harm. In the 2019 election, there was virtually the same level of support for Boris Johnson among the lowest-earning voters as among the rich. As Thomas Frank has shown, the labouring farmers of the American heartlands once voted Democrat, setting themselves against Republican wealthy coastal elites. But then in the second half of the twentieth century, this situation was reversed. Now the flyover states are painted Republican red, with two blue Democrat strips down each coast. Since the public now greets those stubborn problems of poverty and inequality with a mixture of boredom and squeamishness, it's been relatively easy to switch the terms of debate from cash to culture.

According to the political and journalistic orthodoxy, the old polarities are defunct. Left and right have given way to other divisions: on education, age and whether you live in a city or a town. But left versus right is not some kind of party-political dinosaur; it represents the genuinely opposed interests of the 0.01 per cent versus the 99.99 per cent. The 0.01 percenters want to keep their money; everyone else wants it shared out. This opposition is real, and it's ever more urgent; yet in the era of anti-elitism it's being very effectively side-lined.

For centuries, the poor have wielded pitchforks against the rich. But now, the pitchfork-wielders – or pitchfork-as-prop-posers – are demagogues and tech barons like Trump and Jeff Bezos and Peter Thiel and Travis Kalanick. Progressives find it almost unbearably awkward to discuss class and poverty head-on: at the peak of the coronavirus crisis, the footballer Marcus Rashford won a popular campaign for free school meals during the summer holidays in part, I would argue, because he is an embodiment of rags-to-riches success. The currency of oppression has turned to dust in the hands of the left, but it has turned to gold in the hands of the already rich, who apparently need not only all the spoils of society but also an oppression story of their own. They have minted a new currency: that of the non-educated, the looked down-upon, the non-elite, where elite is defined – in Sarah Palin's 2008 formulation – as those who think 'that they are, I guess, better than anyone else'. Being good – as in being fair, looking after the needy, redistributing wealth – is now very bad.

Anti-elitism seems outsiderish, insurgent and disruptive. But who is calling intellectuals, writers and artists 'the elite'? Those who are themselves firmly part of the establishment and economically elite: billionaire real-estate tycoons, Silicon Valley moguls, multinational businessmen and hedge-fund managers who ride in gold lifts and private jets and store their wealth offshore. Thus Betsy DeVos – one of the many Trumpites who like to attack the 'liberal elite' – is said to be worth $2 billion (the DeVos family has an estimated net worth of $5.4 billion), which includes a $10 million vacation home and ten boats, among them a $40 million yacht. Steve Bannon vowed the Trump administration would take America back from 'corporatist, globalist' elites, yet he made his fortune in Hollywood and at Goldman Sachs. The Commerce Secretary, Wilbur Ross, has said, 'We can no longer "coddle" smug elites with special tax breaks,' yet he made his fortune at investment bank Rothschild. The Conservative premier of Ontario, Doug Ford, likes to stand up for the 'little guy' against an elite who, he says, 'drink champagne with their pinkies in the air'. Never mind that he inherited a multi-million-dollar business from his father, the former Toronto mayor, or that he spent years as a city councillor dismantling public services, or that his actual policies support hand-outs to the wealthiest. The wife of the self-styled enemy of the Islington media elite, top PM aide Dominic Cummings, is an editor at *The Spectator*, and they live in Islington.

And there's Trump, of course, and his inner circle of corporate executives, Goldman Sachs bankers and Silicon Valley magnates. And Arron Banks, listed as the director of over forty companies, and worth a reported $240 million, and our friend Farage, who has described his entry into commodities trading thus: 'I ate dozens of oysters, drank champagne cocktails … The solution was found as so many solutions are, on the golf course'; naturally, it helped that 'my father was a well-known character on the Exchange'.

And what about the fortunes of those now branded 'elite'? When I'm out on my bike and pass fellow bookish types on the Camden Town cycle route, they don't look like masters of the universe. They look like the last, slightly frazzled members of a dying breed. Far from being a bloated ruling class, there really aren't many of us left. Newspapers and newsrooms are shedding journalists at a shocking rate. And those who are still clinging desperately to a life of the mind are finding their jobs increasingly deadened by mindless bureaucracy: form-filling, data-entry and the enforced navigation of poorly designed software systems. An envious and punitive managerialism has eroded from the inside the very thing that made these jobs attractive and worthwhile.

In 2016, the author Philip Pullman pointed out that writers don't get paid for appearing at literary festivals – they are supposed to be grateful for the exposure; and are mostly too embarrassed to question it because they still feel somehow residually powerful and well-off. Median earnings for professional writers (those spending more than half their working hours writing) have plummeted by 42 per cent since 2005 to less than £10,500 a year. A 2014 study found that most writers earn less than £600 a year; not surprisingly, the number of authors earning a living solely from their writing dropped from 40 per cent in 2005 to just over 10 per cent by 2013.

A third of freelance journalists earn less than £10,000 per year from their writing; over half of even well-established freelance magazine and newspaper hacks make less than £8,000 a year. Nearly three quarters of artists earn little over a third of the average UK salary from their actual artistic work. Ninety per cent of musicians earn less than £15,000 a year; the majority of that is either slogging around on tour (not practical if you have kids or are over a certain age) or teaching. Very little money is made from music as the actual product: to make a single dollar, an artist's song would need to be played on YouTube nearly 1,500 times. Museum curation jobs are notoriously poorly paid. As for academics, who've had on average seven years of training, more than half of British lecturers – and three quarters of junior staff – are on temporary contracts. Because university lectureships seem the apogee of comfort and luxury – you mean you get to stare out of the window for a living? – the public's heart does not bleed for them. Yet much of my experience of working in universities has been unmanageable workloads, compounded by this false reputation for indolence and entitlement.

The 'elite' slur is associated with middle-class cultural markers – expertise, educational attainment and so on. In fact, 'middle class' has arguably become an even worse insult than 'working class' – to call someone a 'chav' is appalling, yet those who do so are liable to be publicly excoriated. 'Middle class' passes without mention – it's considered somehow deserved. Yet the living standards of the middle classes are now closer to those of the poor than the rich. Since the 1970s and '80s, the 1 per cent, the 0.1 per cent and the 0.01 per cent have seen steep income growth; the top 0.001-ers have seen their pay grow 635 per cent since 1980. By contrast, both low- and middle-income groups have suffered declines in real income since the financial crash, while the costs of housing, childcare and university fees have ballooned. The middle are indeed now squeezed, their former prospects of a life of fulfilling work hobbled by precarious gigs and stagnating wages.

We often hear that the 'liberal elite' has lost touch with its working-class heartlands. Yet while the culture wars have driven them apart, in financial terms the gap between the so-called elite and the working class is narrowing. It's true that many left-wing parties have indeed given up on tackling poverty, although what is usually meant by the 'out of touch' criticism is that left-ists should adopt the values of non-elite communities, which in turn too often means be a little more racist. Pilfering the left-wing critique that economic maximisation has come to dominate everything, the right seek to steer the conversation away from material deprivation and on to cultural values – the objection to Brexit on the grounds of its economic impact is met with the retort: 'It's not just all about money, you know.' While the left are held to a stringent standard of representational literalism – in order to appeal to post-industrial communities, they should look and sound properly northern – Boris Johnson can just wave a fish around in Grimsby. When being an 'ordinary voter' is defined symbolically rather than materially, such performative gestures work.

Back in the days of straightforward class antagonism, the political right defended the interests of the rich and the left stood up for the poor. Those days are gone. Society may be more divided than ever, but now the top aligns itself with the bottom in order to vilify the middle; Hannah Arendt's phrase from *The Origins of Totalitarianism*, 'the temporary alliance of the mob and the elite', aptly describes this marriage of convenience

– convenient, at least, for the super-rich. Pinstriped spivs and mockney financiers have appealed to disgruntled white van men, nationalist black-cab drivers and Tommy Robinson acolytes. It's an intimidating combination of money and muscle, underpinned by an ersatz sense of moral and political reparation. What we are seeing now, in fact, is not so much the oft-repeated opposition between populists and elites as the new phenomenon of elite populism: the real elites pretending to side with the people.

Four

'Private Opulence and
Public Squalor'

JUST AS WE'VE been persuaded that politicians, thinkers and cultural practitioners are enjoying elite status, we're told that universities, theatres, broadcasters and galleries are relatively comfortable: tightening their belts, perhaps, but this is only to be expected at a time of austerity; and what about those opera houses confident enough to charge £200 a ticket? The former Universities Minister David Willetts criticises higher education for exerting 'producer-power' at the expense of consumer interests, erecting a 'tiresome barrier' to market competition. The MailOnline calls the BBC the British Bloated Corporation; *The Sun*'s Dan

Wootton is glad that 'the bloated BBC is finally sipping expensive champagne in a last-chance saloon surrounded by Corbynista socialists'. At last, he wrote in early 2020, it looks set to get its comeuppance for serving only the interests of 'the London remoaning media elite'.

The Palace of Westminster is crumbling, local authorities are at breaking point and arts and culture organisations are pared to the bone. The Arts Council's budget has been cut by 30 per cent since 2010, and it has reduced its grants to the Royal Opera House, the Southbank Centre, the Royal Shakespeare Company and the National Theatre. Almost £400 million has been cut from local authority arts budgets over the past decade: local government funding for culture in the UK is almost the lowest in Europe. The proportion of its GDP that the UK spends on the arts is less than half that of France.

In 1996 in the US, the budget for the National Endowment for the Arts was halved. As of 2014, only 4 per cent of all arts funding in America comes from public sources. Donald Trump has proposed eliminating the National Endowment for the Arts altogether, along with the National Endowment for the Humanities. In Australia, there has been 70 per cent less funding for artists since 2014. At the end of 2019, Australia's conservative government got rid of the Federal Ministry for the Arts altogether.

And that's before we even get on to the devastation wrought by Covid-19. At the time of writing, the entire British performing arts industry, along with our museums and galleries, faces a grave, even existential threat. With the basic functions of the state under such strain, it's become harder than ever to argue that the apparently 'optional' arts are actually essential.

As the arts and humanities face long-term starvation, STEM is on the rise. Since 2011, government funding for the humanities in the UK has been withdrawn at the undergraduate level; STEM support remains. Humanities funding in the US has been falling since 2009: it's now on average less than half of 1 per cent of funding for science and engineering. The trend is global: in India, a great tradition of humanities education is being replaced by business and technology. If education is no longer valued intrinsically on its own terms, but only in terms of earnings prospects, the humanities become perceived as pointless excess. This is despite the fact that a lot of science is wonderfully abstract. Scientific knowledge is also under threat by the anti-elite brigade. But the main target is the humanities and those who have studied them. In 1965, President Lyndon Johnson signed the National Endowment for the Arts and the National Endowment for the Humanities into existence, along with a set of other ambitious social programmes, under the rubric of the Great Society. 'Somehow,' he observed in his speech, 'the scientists always seem to get the penthouse, while the arts and the humanities get the basement.' This dominance proceeds almost without comment now.

The privileging of science over the arts and humanities, therefore, and not even science, but narrowly pragmatic branches of technology, business and vocational service-sector training, is an insidious aspect of the reductionist utilitarianism cheapening our world. The humanities enrich us in ways that do not readily translate into cash metrics. And there's another reason they're valuable, and another reason they are under attack:

because they have the capacity to challenge the status quo. Whereas science is about knowledge, the humanities are also about critique. And this is why reactionary and philistine governments want to shut them down.

In Austerity Britain, where talk of straitened times and balancing the books has been thoroughly internalised – even, or especially, by those who are themselves struggling financially – it is hard to really feel the plenitude we in reality enjoy as the sixth richest country in the world. The economic outlook post-Covid is bleak, but corporate bailouts are apparently still available: in the form, for instance, of a \$170 billion tax cut to American real-estate tycoons. We live in an age of what John Kennedy Galbraith called 'private opulence and public squalor'. As Nicholas Shaxson, James Henry and Gabriel Zucman have noted, the global super-rich have up to \$35 trillion squirrelled away in offshore accounts, depriving governments of hundreds of billions each year in tax revenues. Privatised electricity, gas, water and rail companies pay out £12 billion a year to investors and shareholders. A single corporation, Amazon, is worth \$880 billion. Corporate profits in the United States are nearly \$8 trillion dollars per year; UK companies make about £400 billion a year. In comparison, total government spending on education is £85 billion a year. As Franklin Roosevelt put it, 'Plenty is at our doorstep, but a generous use of it languishes in the very sight of the supply.'

The new philistinism proceeds under the guise of a false expediency. We the public are encouraged to participate in a grand cognitive dissonance, politely averting our eyes from the vast luxury apartment developments springing up all over London and the south-east, while agreeing that, in straitened times, spending on higher education, the arts and culture is an indulgence we can no longer afford. Such fripperies are always put up against the poorest and neediest in society in a shaming hierarchy of priorities, where they will always lose; they are never set against yacht design or penthouse construction or corporate air travel. A kind of get-with-the-programme realism is attached to private profligacy as well as public penury: you think the billionaires are going to magically redistribute some of their spare cash to the arts? Welcome to the real world!

It's not just budgets that are shrinking; it's influence

too. In the past, a humanities education – particularly in
the classics – would have been the valued foundation of
a respected career in public life. The Labour politicians
Roy Jenkins, Anthony Crosland and Denis Healey all
had intellectual hinterlands: Jenkins, a son and grandson
of Welsh miners, wrote a series of political biographies,
Crosland was an author and former Oxford don, and
Healey a photographer and poet. Prior to the last decades of the twentieth century, it was commonplace for
politicians to have a thorough knowledge of history and
cite past precedents in their speeches.

That all changed in the 1980s and 1990s. Anthony
Sampson, Jeremy Paxman, Andrew Adonis and Stephen
Pollard – and, from a more leftist perspective, Owen
Jones and Aeron Davis – have all documented the same
story: that traditional, establishment institutions have
been replaced by a new, abrasive culture of business
and banking. Power is now located in the City and its
global financial network. Graduates who might once
have been destined for public service now troop off to
do their MBAs or are hoovered up by the university
'milk round' and funnelled into finance and management

consultancy; for those careers, a humanities degree is nothing more than a quaint diversion.

Despite being a socialist, I'm also a bit of an old conservative; because conservatives used to value, well, conservatism. But now, a new generation of Tory radicals is as aggressive towards the old establishment as it is towards organised labour. In the process, it's created, as Paxman puts it, 'another elite, a new moneyed caste'. I'm not saying the old bastions of the monarchy, the church and the army were necessarily that benign or beneficial, but at least many of their ranks were informed by ideas as well as cash; and even if the establishment didn't always operate in the public interest, at least it resided in the public rather than the private sphere. I'm not calling for the restoration of the old boys' network, but rather the reinvention of Enlightenment values – this time energised by a radical commitment to equity and underpinned by rigorous standards.

Five

'Democratisation' and the Culture Wars

NOT ONLY HAVE the populist right convinced the public that cultural institutions and universities – even, pre-Covid, the NHS – are awash with cash, they've also created the widespread impression that the arts, the media and higher education are synonymous with elite privilege. And because they are considered a luxury, these institutions feel the need to show that they are useful in order to receive any funding at all. The BBC, the National Theatre and the Royal Opera House are routinely hectored about taking on more diverse staff and talent, yet there's a comparative public silence when it comes to having more BAME people on the payroll of corporate behemoths.

There is much talk, therefore, of 'democratising' the arts, journalism, universities and the publishing and music industries. Even while budgets are squeezed more than ever, they are pressured by neo-Maoist ministers and highly paid senior managers to 'justify' the use of taxpayers' and students' money by acting as social workers, performing acts of social and cultural reparation and putting on a show of promoting inclusion and diversity.

The real elites have transposed the problem of economic inequality onto the conveniently figurative realms of culture and education, enabling astronomical profiteering to be concealed while hard-pressed theatre groups, struggling galleries and faltering newspapers are hammered with the punitive tasks of outreach and community 'impact'. Because these realms are so concerned with visibility and optics, it's easy to demonstrate that equality and diversity are being achieved; but only in a superficial, role-modelled fashion. This approach fits right in to a world where appearance matters more than substance, where screen-based, social media-fuelled, publicity-driven surface impression trumps reality. The actual structure of society remains largely unchanged. Productivity is plummeting and our manufacturing industry is rusting away, but instead of addressing the problem of what we are *doing* as a country economically, and bridging the north–south divide meaningfully, arts centres, museums and arms of the BBC are simply plonked down in deprived areas: let them eat culture!

Democratisation, outreach, impact: these have the ring of a social good, but they are actually the flipside of monetary measurement: as the phrase 'public accountability' indicates, this is also about accountancy, about bean-counting. The requirement to 'account for yourself' indicates a lack of legitimacy, as if you have to justify your existence. Forcing arts and culture organisations to be socially useful and 'engage new audiences' is an unquestioned good to many right-thinking people, but I believe it undermines their core purpose and imposes burdens on them that they are hard pressed to fulfil. The point of these bodies should be to make great art and great culture, and to create and disseminate the highest forms of knowledge. It should not be to solve social problems that are the rightful preserve of governments and the state. By making culture, education and journalism into public relations arenas for tackling inequality, politics has given up on trying to improve society in any kind of organised way.

At the very same time that right-wing politicians have been cutting arts and education budgets, therefore, they have tasked them with dealing with the social and economic inequality that has been abandoned as a policy priority. There's a connection here with the culture wars: the transposing of political debates onto shibboleths of cultural identity, and their deployment as weapons in a disavowed and sublimated political campaign. What is supposed to matter these days is not whether you are right-wing or left-wing, but what are your *values* – whether, say, you are pro- or anti-gay marriage. And political allegiance is now drawn along the lines of education, not money. This enables an alliance between the uneducated rich and the uneducated poor against a shrinking educated middle class. And it enables politicians to imagine that by calling for increased access to degree courses or plays at the National Theatre they are bridging what is now falsely identified as the important new social divide, rather than addressing real, gaping, financial disparity.

I hear more about recruiting 'diverse' writers, journalists and actors than I hear about the need to maintain quality. This is of course not to say that having properly representative cultural participants is anathema to quality, or that it is not an important goal in itself. But as with socio-economic inequality, we shirk systemic solutions to discrimination while at the same time tasking our already stretched and threadbare cultural sector with the job of publicly performing racial and gender equality.

We create a society that is materially unequal, but those who get clobbered about diversity and representation are at the very end of the food chain. It's a little hard to get equal numbers of women as men onto *Start the Week*, say, when fewer women are writing books and giving high-profile public lectures, because they've not had the economic wherewithal and the social circumstances to get on and achieve those goals. These are deep structural factors that arts and media organisations have little capacity to alter.

The left are barking up the wrong tree with their overwhelming emphasis on identity politics. Interminable injunctions to 'check your privilege' overlook the fact that the really rich and powerful would never bother with such fastidious self-scrutiny. In the 'era' of #MeToo, individual white male Hollywood producers come to represent the problem, rather than broader disparities. I'm not saying that race, gender and sexuality don't matter, or don't correlate to other more material forms of inequality. But let's put the big-picture power analysis back into all these debates.

A glance at the funding guidance published by Arts Council England (ACE) illustrates the tendency I'm talking about. Anyone seeking support for their exhibition, ballet or book has to demonstrate, exhaustively, 'whether access and diversity have been considered effectively', whether their project exhibits 'inclusivity and relevance', if it constitutes 'public engagement' and delivers 'civic and social benefits'. ACE's vision is not restricted to supporting the arts: 'We want to see communities that are more socially cohesive and economically robust', it says, 'in which residents experience improved physical and mental wellbeing as a result of investment in culture.' In a section on its website entitled 'Why art and culture matters', ACE lists the key 'facts': 'Art and culture contributes £10.6 billion to the UK economy', and 'Arts and culture help tackle social injustice'. It's not really ACE's fault: the injunction to prove social value is imposed top-down by government ministers; but it's a dispiritingly instrumental rationale nonetheless.

In its 57-page funding guidance to big museums, applicants are instructed to 'show how you are sharing your work with as large and wide an audience as possible, especially with those who are currently least-engaged with arts and culture'. Museums must have 'equality plans' which focus on at least two of the following 'protected characteristics' defined by the Equalities Act: 'age; disability; gender reassignment; marriage and civil partnership; pregnancy and maternity; race; religion or belief; sex; and sexual orientation', as well as 'class/socio-economic status'. There's also a persistent demand across the ACE's funding literature that arts organisations should be 'child-centred':

museums, for example, should 'provide inspiring and relevant opportunities that stretch, challenge and excite children and young people', which will not only 'foster positive dispositions towards the arts' but also 'enhance their self-esteem, wider aspirations and life and career choices'. Just putting on a good exhibition or play is no longer enough.

ACE does emphasise quality and excellence in its guidance, but it does so in curiously apologetic terms. 'Excellence' is defined as 'providing high-quality arts work and experiences to achieve the best possible outcomes for children and young people'. Excellence is rarely mentioned without being linked to social outcomes and audience engagement. In its most recent ten-year strategy, published in 2010, ACE defined its mission as being to 'support the arts and cultural sector to pursue excellence in all it does' – 'by which we mean', it rushed to clarify, 'the creation of work of artistic and cultural excellence and the way this work engages with audiences'.

Ten years on and even this cautious definition has been watered down. The emphasis in the latest consultation document, published in 2019, has shifted from 'arts and culture' to people expressing their own creativity and developing 'their own creative potential'. In 2010, there were eighteen mentions of 'excellence'; in 2019, just four. 'We do not consider that certain types or scales of artistic activity are inherently of higher quality or value than others,' the document states; 'excellence can just as readily be found in a village hall as a concert hall – in both the process of participation and in the work that is produced.'

The equivalent funding body north of the border, Creative Scotland, does state that creativity 'challenges us, entertains us and makes us think', but also that it makes society better: it 'makes an invaluable contribution to our health and wellbeing – both physically and mentally', 'opens our minds to cultural diversity and social inclusion', and improves 'social mobility'. The Heritage Lottery Fund, meanwhile, places great emphasis on 'outcomes', defined as 'a result of what your project does. It's a change that happens, rather than an activity or service you provide', the guidance states.

Outcomes are different from outputs: 'the output

of cooking dinner is a plate of food. But the outcome is a full and satisfied person,' the document clarifies. 'Project outcomes are really important to us because we want to back projects that make a difference, rather than projects that just make some stuff,' they say. 'Just make some stuff': the impatience with art for art's sake is palpable. A 'mandatory' outcome for grants is widening participation: 'if your project is a success, then the range of people benefiting from heritage will be more diverse than before your project started', in terms of 'a broader range of ages, ethnicities and social backgrounds, more disabled people, or groups who have never engaged with your heritage before'. Other outcomes to be demonstrated include 'greater wellbeing': 'participants will report, for example, increased happiness, greater satisfaction, reduced levels of anxiety, and/or that life feels more worthwhile as a result of their involvement in your project'.

I realise I'm being a bit hard on these promoters and upholders of the arts. They are themselves responding to government stipulations. I'm also not saying that all public art is bad. But why can't a piece of art be valuable in itself, as a delicious plate of food? Yes, we should take steps to widen access to those art works – but as a society the best way to do that is to address the material problems of overwork and low pay that deny people the leisure time necessary to appreciate culture. The pressure we put on artists themselves is a symptom of that collective failure to take action further up the food chain.

Arts funding has become the reward not straightforwardly for brilliance but for fulfilling a bureaucratic exercise that makes reductive and often contrived claims about widening access. Post-it note feedback boards in galleries are rife: please take a moment to tell us about your experience. Audience participation in theatrical productions has become commonplace: recent examples of the latter include Richard Bean's *One Man, Two Guvnors*, James Graham's *Privacy*, and Kevin Toolis's *The Confessions of Gordon Brown*; not to mention the huge immersive theatre scene pioneered by Punchdrunk and dreamthinkspeak. My beef is not with the many radical and challenging experiments in puncturing the fourth wall but with the spurious claims that are often made for its social utility. Research grants are predicated on community impact. Arts practitioners and lecturers spend their working hours filling applications and reports with grey guff about participation that they don't believe in and perhaps nobody properly reads. Gaming and box-ticking are rife. Just as anti-elitism functions as a smokescreen for the rank inequality destroying our society, cultural 'democratisation' is a meretricious substitute for economic justice and political representation.

Six

The Great Capitulation

TTACKS BY THE alt-right are bad enough,
but what I find really depressing is the way
liberals have lost their backbone. Normally
confident adults are terrified to say in public what
they really feel – about Brexit and culture alike. With
their worth constantly weighed against the most press-
ing social priorities, arts organisations no longer seem
convinced by their own right to exist, while those who
thrive on their output are tongue-tied. Dyed-in-the-
wool politicians, authors and traditional journalists are
all tiptoeing around, commenting glumly that 'perhaps
we've had our day', or if they are privately convinced
that what they are doing is worthwhile, they neverthe-
less keep their heads down for fear of being excoriated

on social media. Those who research the archives, write brilliant novels, test our water, food and medicines and represent our interests in Parliament seventy hours a week find themselves unable to defend what they do on principle. The new anti-elitism is hitting home.

Our culture, in fact, is undergoing a curious bifurcation: one branch is heading towards worthy social work, the other towards trashy, brash Americana. The so-called liberal elite, with their backs against the wall, can't defend anything without resorting to either a dreary and spurious functional justification or to lowest common denominator market demand. It's grey community centre or game show bling. On one hand, progressives have become weakly complicit in the right's imposition of utilitarian rationales on cultural and intellectual endeavour. On the other, I agree, uncharacteristically, with *The Sun*'s attack-dog commentator Dan Wootton when he points out that BBC websites shouldn't be posting clickbait about *Love Island* – a service well covered by other online outlets.

The neo-Maoist attack on cultural excellence is coming from the 'radical' right, therefore, but it's also being enabled by an enfeebled left. While the right use cultural populism to disguise their socio-economic agenda, the left no longer have the language or the confidence with which to advocate for intrinsic merit. The right promote barbarian philistinism as inevitable, even moral, and progressives defend an educational culture where although everyone is tested constantly we feel unable to tell anyone that they are less than awesome. Well-meaning primary schools tie themselves in knots trying to reconcile an insanely detailed and exacting assessment regime with a saccharine refusal to say any story or performance is better than any other. Schools operate a careful rota of 'star of the week' certificates so every child gets a go. My kids even have a sheet of stickers from a pound-shop activity book with the slogans 'Well done!', 'Great homework!' and 'You're brilliant!' Just as the gold standard of praise has given way to hyperinflation, the principle of teachers' authority has been undermined. Non-hierarchical techniques such as 'flipped learning' and 'teaching from the back of the room' are in vogue. Pedagogical guides for teachers and lecturers recommend replacing the sage on the stage with the guide on the side. This is deeply confusing for children, who are being raised in an atmosphere of intense neoliberal competition combined with misconceived attempts to ensure parity.

The participants of the famous caucus-race in Lewis Carroll's *Alice's Adventures in Wonderland* run randomly around in all directions; when they ask the Dodo to determine the winner, he announces that 'everybody has won and all must have prizes'. We are similarly unable to determine cultural or educational merit. There was once a single literary prize of note: the Booker, founded in 1969. Now there are prizes not only for women's fiction but for writers evoking a sense of place, for experimental fiction and international writing, for poetry, prose, history, biography, nature writing, political satire and crime, for debut authors and independent presses.

In 2017, Amazon launched the Kindle UK Storyteller Award for self-published authors, explaining that readers, alongside 'literary experts', 'will play a significant role in the competition', with the award shortlist decided partly by 'customer interest'. It's not surprising that a tech giant such as Amazon would have a vested interest in eroding existing forms of critical authority. But the traditional cultural establishment itself is becoming ever more diffident. In 2019, the Booker Prize was awarded to two authors, and the four nominees for that year's Turner Prize asked the judges to give the award collectively to all of them, 'in the name of commonality, multiplicity and solidarity'. It sounds warm and friendly, but it signifies a loss of confidence in critical judgement and undermines the prize's prestige.

Britain's traditionally world-leading system of higher education is being comprehensively trashed: universities are letting in posh students with rock-bottom A levels, and grade inflation is rampant. I'm not against increasing university enrolments, but if the reading diet of a typical Glaswegian 'factory girl' in the early nineteenth century would put most contemporary undergraduates to shame, then what's the point? The expansion of higher education is a sham if the degrees aren't worth the paper they're written on. Universities can't decide if they want to be elite or not. They boast of their ability to turn down all but the best applicants, yet at the same time emphasise their inclusivity and the allowances they make for students who need help with basic writing skills.

At a university where I once taught, we had an induction day for new master's students. The room was packed with enthusiastic new recruits, all palpably excited to have been granted admission to such a prestigious course. But halfway through the session, the course leader started asking if there was any feedback or complaints about the course so far. I felt the energy drain from the room. Instead of being challenged to meet the university's high expectations, students suddenly realised the university was bending over backwards to meet their needs. We might think that simply meeting students' needs makes them happy. They may think that themselves. But we, and they, are wrong. We are happy when we do something well, in a rigorous institution with elevated expectations, and when our achievement is meaningfully recognised.

The vilification of baby boomers is an increasingly active ingredient in the anti-expert anti-elitism corroding our world. In the past, the young would rail against the old. They would stick it to the man. The old held their ground: you too will grow old, they said. Now, the old have capitulated to the young. Mea culpa, they admit. What do we know? The old guard are diving head-first off their pedestals, second-guessing what they think young people want. 'As commercials got people used to absorbing information quickly, I had to change my style to give them more jump cuts or they'd be bored,' said the late TV drama producer Quinn Martin in 1983. 'The whole art form has speeded up.' A promenade performance of *A Midsummer Night's Dream* encourages audiences to groove, awkwardly, to Beyoncé.

Traditional media organisations are performing ever more embarrassing displays of dad-dancing to try to appeal to a younger audience. The BBC's most recent annual plan states as a priority to 'step up our commitment to better serve young audiences'; it already has *Snog Marry Avoid?* and *Glow Up*, hosted by Stacey Dooley, 'which sees ten aspiring make-up artists compete to be named Britain's next make-up star'. If they stuck to what they are good at, those young people would respect them and come to them in time. We are accepting youthful iconoclasm at face value. It's like

Henry IV Part 1 without *Part 2*. Hal has humiliated Falstaff, and he never grows up. The meek valorising of the views of young people is part of the same impulse as the instinctive privileging of the views of 'ordinary people' – even if they are misinformed. We think it's respectful, but it's actually the opposite: yes, sure, whatever you say, even if it's wrong. Generational financial disparity partly explains this tendency, but the economic is being confused with the cultural. The guiltily instinctive deferral to Generation Z downgrades knowledge, and it effaces the struggle for genuine political enfranchisement and social equality.

The bullying attack on 'experts', cultural figures, academics and journalists is also directed at politicians, the political system and the welfare state. Those who represent us at the highest level, and provide social security to the most vulnerable, are maligned as condescending do-gooders. Centrist Labour MPs Liz Kendall and Steve Reed have said that too many public services assume a 'parent–child relationship' with clients. The populist right's disparagement of the 'political establishment' and the top-down state is unwittingly echoed, therefore, by

progressives: both sides rally their supporters by defining themselves in opposition to a political 'elite'. In fact,
the left are even more squeamish, because they confuse
being socially egalitarian with abolishing authority in
institutions and in the political system itself. Campaign-
ing groups which have traditionally been devoted to
addressing economic injustice in the population at large
are currently squandering their energies trying to abol-
ish hierarchies in their own organisational culture. While
it's important to be vigilant and self-reflexive, there's a
danger that in doing so they jump straight into the trap
laid for them by the populist right, who wish to clear
radical campaigners from the field of mainstream politics and erode public support for our political system;
which for all its faults is the only mechanism we have
for bringing about a more equitable world.

The expenses crisis of 2009 exemplified these counterproductive attacks on politics and politicians. The
freedom of information campaigner Heather Brooke
described the exposure of the scandal as a 'victory' for
the people over Parliament and its 'elitist attitude': those
'right honourable gentlemen' who'd turned their noses

up at the public 'lower down'. Yet the effect was to distract us all from broader injustices. The expenses scandal blew up immediately after the financial crash: public outrage over claims for bath plugs that cost 88p functioned as a safety valve for anger at the £850 billion spent bailing out the banks. Since then, this supposedly comfortable 'elite' has been the victim of mass trolling, rape threats and even murder.

From the NSA's Edward Snowden to Li Wenliang, the Wuhan doctor who warned about the Covid-19 pandemic, whistleblowers have demonstrated that sunshine, as Justice Louis Brandeis put it, is the best disinfectant. But while concealment can cushion unaccountable power, it can also be a thin-skinned clench. As those who have worked in an open-plan office know all too well, zealous calls for transparency can result in even more secrecy and distortion of the truth as workers – and governments – apply their efforts to making what they do look good. Winners work the system; losers are victims of circumstance; most simply go through the motions. League tables produce sink schools; academics spend research time on research assessment exercises.

Professionals, experts and public administrators alike rely on shared codes, technical shorthand and evolved techniques for complex decision-making: necessary, but often lost in translation. As Lawrence Lessig has argued in an essay for the *New Republic*, 'Against Transparency', when it comes to policy detail the public have shorter attention spans than politicians, and this leads to damaging misunderstandings. It's not that the public 'isn't smart enough to figure out what the truth is', Lessig writes. On the contrary: 'The public is too smart to waste its time focusing on matters that are not important for it to understand. The ignorance here is rational, not pathological.' Yet it leads us to jump to unflattering conclusions and assume the worst. We may come to realise too late that the democratic institutions we were led to despise are actually the imperfect but necessary bulwarks that protect us from arbitrary power.

Seven

How They Get Away
With It

TODAY'S GOLIATHS PRETEND to be Davids
– or the Davids' true friends. The populist
right and their corporate counterparts, the
new pseudo-entrepreneurial, 'disruptive' business
behemoths, are secretly wedded to the principle of
winner-takes-all monopoly, but they hide it behind a
pervasive rhetoric of egalitarianism and the breaking-
open of the old establishment. 'Over the years, a
revolution has been taking place,' says Robin Ryde,
a consultant and author of *Never Mind the Bosses: Has-
tening the Death of Deference for Business Success*. 'It
is best described as a consistent decline in the level of

deference paid to authority.' Issuing as it so often does from the mouths of reactionary politicians, management strategists and tech moguls, this kind of iconoclasm is neither radical nor empowering.

As Martin Gurri has noted in his book *The Revolt of the Public*, the new platforms for expression have provided an outlet for verbalising anger. But that hasn't manifested in material social change, because electoral politics has been taken over by reactionaries. Apps like Twitter may create the impression that the disenfranchised are 'having their say', but it doesn't make any meaningful difference in the real world. And in the meantime, the opened floodgates of online information have prompted a backlash against the institutions that represent us, inform us and keep us safe: Parliament, news organisations, universities. These 'public' bodies have been subjected to forensic scrutiny and have haemorrhaged trust, while the private sphere remains blissfully immune. From Lord Hutton's investigation to the internal Savile inquiry, the BBC has endured waves of bruising humiliation; while some is deserved, the overall effect is the weakening of news media. The salaries of presenters and university vice-chancellors have been subjected to intense probing; again, this is sometimes appropriate, but it reinforces the false impression of comfortable opulence. Right-wing populists have turned public anger about unfairness against the very individuals and institutions whose job it is to ensure fairness. So the vicious circle perpetuates itself, and the 'solution' the public have found to their anger makes their lives worse, and fuels their anger further.

These false solutions have been incubated and propagated in Silicon Valley by Bezos, Musk, Brin and the rest, with their carefully curated casual uniform of T-shirt, jeans and trainers. 'The Internet is Under New Management: Yours', Yahoo tells us, and Vodafone's slogan is 'Power to You'. Those who dominate society do so now by very visibly showcasing their apparently citizen-centric or ethical credentials. Luxury housing developments on green belts are waved through on the promise of a few 'affordable' units or a doctor's surgery; the Gates empire combats malaria; grammar school expansion is justified using a pledge to increase social mobility; airports sponsor school children to plant trees.

There's a new name for this kind of behaviour: 'woke capitalism', but as I described in my 2012 book *Get Real*, it's been going on for a few decades. Variously known as 'cuddly capitalism', greenwash and astroturf, this kind of window-dressing lends street cred to the super-rich.

Just as inequality is hidden behind the façade of heavily promoted role models, struggling gig workers are supposed to be content with the unlikely prospect of becoming a YouTube bedroom star. The tech megacorps are acting as a kind of vast alchemical processing plant, melting down the real, material culture of newspapers and books and records and CDs into a digital, fungible soup, and at the same time diverting the issue of economic inequality onto the false dawn of 'pro-am' democratisation. They are turning culture into money and money into culture.

The real culprits, we are told, are not plutocrats, but cultural 'gatekeepers'. In 2018, Mark Zuckerberg posted a note on his Facebook profile. 'Many of us got into technology because we believe it can be a democratizing force for putting power in people's hands,' he wrote. 'I believe the world is better when more people have a voice to share their experiences, and when traditional gatekeepers like governments and media companies don't control what ideas can be expressed.' And here is Google's Eric Schmidt:

> A decade ago, to launch a digital music service, you prob-
> ably would have enlisted a handful of elite tastemakers
> to pick the hottest new music … Today, you're much
> better off building a smart system that can learn from
> the real world – what actual listeners are most likely to
> like next – and help you predict who and where the next
> Adele might be.

There you have it: the replacement of curation with market forces, justified by a spurious levelling of the playing field.

Co-opting the progressive language of social justice, digital oligarchs insist that the old arbiters – in music and art, journalism and politics – must give way to the wisdom of the crowd. Pseudo-progressive bunk about horizontalism, the age of the amateur and placing the means of production in users' hands legitimates the biggest power-grab of money and information the world has ever seen. It's curious how people are so scornful of authority in this area, in fact, when the Hansard Society's Audit of Political Engagement has found that when it comes to Prime Ministers, 54 per cent of Britons say they'd be quite happy with a 'strong leader'.

Those Californian tech geeks have acted on their jealousy about the attractive and glamorous reputation of the arts, media and humanities by taking a scythe to those delicate ecosystems of lunches and launches and conferences and industry norms and unspoken rules. They've been bolstered by science popularisers and sociobiologists such as the cognitive psychologist Steven Pinker, the primatologist Frans de Waal, or the physicist Brian Cox, who is keen to stress that – on the level of 'basic biochemistry' at least – we are barely distinguishable from a blade of grass. The idea that humans are special, superior to so-called lower forms of life is, he says, 'an emergent illusion created by the sheer complexity of our arrangement of atoms'. I have no problem with scientific knowledge per se, but evangelical popular scientists like Cox – while eschewing religion – make science into a kind of faith (the watchword is 'wonder'), with him playing the role of high priest. The stated enemy may be religion, but the real opposition to this kind of deterministic reductionism is the humanities. We have devalued our own human capacity for making and discerning beautiful or difficult things by dumbing ourselves down to the level of robots and algorithms. Literature, music, art, journalism, education, expertise and authority are all being degraded by the metrics of markets and machines and corroded by the universal acid of neo-Darwinism, competition and digitisation.

In his 2001 book *Emergence*, Steven Johnson described how many aspects of our world – from slime mould to the formation of modern city neighbourhoods – are created bottom-up rather than top-down – relying on 'masses of relatively stupid elements, rather than a single, intelligent "executive branch"'. We've moved from description from prescription: this model has become the defining paradigm for our world. But in reality, the thriving hubbub of mid-range artists and institutions has been replaced not by an autonomous multitude of ants on the ground but by that multitude combined with a super-powerful puppeteer at the top, pulling the strings and reaping the rewards.

Everywhere you look, from culture to education to politics, reducing standards is reclassified as being fair to ordinary people and giving them a voice. The bottom-up, the grassroots and the ultra-local are popular buzz-words. Take higher education, where marketisation has replaced quality and thoughtful scholarship and knowledge in its own right, and students have been weaponised against beleaguered lecturers, slyly por-trayed as a cosy cabal ripe for a take-down. Student complaints about poor 'value for money' are levelled at those who teach them, rather than at government min-isters or senior managers, the real architects of the new system. According to the business-friendly University Alliance, academia's reluctance to emphasise 'employ-ability' carries 'more than a whiff of snobbery'. It is 'business' that's now regarded as the ally of ordinary people, in contrast to 'entitled' academics who presume their role is to impart knowledge for its own sake. The right-wing think tank Policy Exchange criticises uni-versities for their 'sneering' attitude. To even criticise market consumerism now is considered elitist. The virtually unchallenged mantra in modern academia is 'open access': the notion that publicly funded research should be made almost instantaneously available to the public – whether or not they actually have a burning interest in the ecclesiastical history of sixteenth-century Scotland – yet this is destroying both the mechanisms for maintaining impartial scholarly standards and the funding model for publishing academic books, which are the professionally agreed currency unit of research.

To be a lecturer in a British university these days is to be treated like a kind of miscreant service provider, buried by bureaucracy and hectored constantly by sometimes overtly hostile managers. Students are now customers, as sensitive as flowers and simultaneously ferociously demanding: if corporations were as in thrall to customer feedback as universities are to the National Student Survey, we'd all be living in a consumer heaven. Of course, it's not the students' fault; it's hell for young people too: their spiralling mental health crisis is met with tick-box student support and increasingly automated wellbeing 'services'; and once they leave behind the solicitous, tell-us-your-views embrace of higher education, they step off the cliff of the post-work future. They are being set against the lecturers in a fruitless struggle between two types of put-upon victim by university managers unable to fully enjoy their exponential salaries because they are under the cosh of government targets.

And as with academia, so with TV. Sky's James Murdoch denounces public service broadcasting as 'authoritarian' and 'creationist' compared with the supposedly more people-centred 'Darwinism' of the free market. Rule by algorithms and aggregation is given a millennial, grassroots spin. Discernment has given way to data. There was a time when market populism was associated with brash profit. Now it has been redefined as a kind of socialism. The right-wing think tank the Institute of Economic Affairs has hosted an event on 'Privatising the BBC – From Public Service Broadcasting to Broadcasting Serving the Public'. The original principle has been inverted. Likewise, public support for the arts used to mean top-down grants; now it's the public buying tickets. Individual human judgement and an idealistic belief in collective solidarity have given way to mass judgement and narcissistic individualism.

Patrician BBC mandarins and presenters like John Reith and Kenneth Clark once defended high culture against the forces of modern barbarianism. Now their private school- and Oxbridge-educated counterparts like Sir Peter Bazalgette and *Downton Abbey* writer Lord Fellowes promote the culturally populist media agenda. It's the worst of all worlds: social exclusivity and trash TV.

There used to be an opposition between 'high' and 'low' culture; now high culture is proscribed in the name of inclusivity. Yet this has the opposite impact to what was intended: it effectively denies that the masses are able to grasp anything challenging or avant-garde. It's actually top-down curation that respects the capacities of the ordinary viewer or reader.

The working classes are automatically associated with the market, with materialism, populism and commercialism – yet, as we will go on to see, this is a relatively new, entirely subjective and hugely insulting idea.

Eight

Excellence Is Not Privilege

T HE POPULIST RIGHT conflate cultural excellence, the media and political office with social and economic privilege – and they are able to do so because in practice, nowadays, those qualities do often go hand in hand. Yet this is the result of specific historical and political factors, and not a natural, logical state of affairs. Take culture and the media first of all. Half of all top British actors are privately educated. Tom Hiddleston, Eddie Redmayne, Damian Lewis and Dominic West all went to Eton. From James Blunt to Florence Welch, Lily Allen to Chris Martin, privately educated artists also dominate the music industry. Fifty-four per cent of the top 100 newspaper editors, columnists, broadcasters and executives went to fee-paying schools, way more than the national average of 7 per cent. With media industries shrinking, practically the only way to get in is to be the son or daughter of an already prominent columnist or presenter. Well into the twenty-first century, in the supposed age of meritocracy, we are seeing the crystallisation of new dynasties – the progeny of film stars taking on the family mantle.

The same is happening in politics. An uncomfortable number are children of the leading lights of a previous generation – Stephen Kinnock, Ed Miliband, Hilary Benn. Too many MPs did PPE at Oxford, and too many are disproportionately wealthy. Boris Johnson, his brother Jo Johnson, David Cameron, Jacob Rees-Mogg and Oliver Letwin – all are Old Etonians.

In 1979, 16 per cent of MPs had a background in manual work; in 2010, the proportion had dropped to 4 per cent. The rise of the professional, well-off politician is the product of specific circumstances, the result of neoliberal policies that have concentrated wealth and power at the top, compromised social mobility and weakened working-class representation. Politics has become technocratic and professionalised through the spad entry route, managerialism, commercial influence and the revolving door between ministerial office and business. As Max Weber observed, if you don't want the modern democratic state to be run by people of independent wealth, 'one must pay people highly and provide them with a pension'.

MPs have become socially homogenous and detached, therefore, but there's no intrinsic reason why there should be such a thing as a 'political class'. The word 'elite' means privileged, but it comes originally from the Latin 'eligere', to 'elect': 'elite' also just means those who are elected. Right-wing populism elides the two. Just because those in power tend to come from a privileged background (the elect few) it doesn't mean there's something inherently wrong with the idea of holding political office; but the populist right and left alike throw the baby out with the bathwater.

As John Gray argues, we have extrapolated the idea of automatic cumulative progress from science into every other area of human civilisation. This distracts us from the very many instances where the clock is running backwards. We unthinkingly assume that bastions of privilege are artefacts of the past. There's a common perception that the traditional old boys' network is now finally breaking down. But this is not necessarily the case. Although these dynasties and establishment set-ups have historical roots, they were radically challenged in the nineteenth and twentieth centuries. When people bemoan the centralisation of cultural capital in London and the south-east, it's almost as if the stupendous neoclassical grandeur of Victorian civic architecture in Preston or Leeds or Sunderland never actually existed.

If we trace the relationship between cultural status and social status, we find that it has actually fluctuated through history. In the medieval period, feudal hierarchies were in place, but there was a clear path via the apprenticeship system to becoming a journeyman and finally a master craftsman. That system gradually broke down in the seventeenth and eighteenth centuries, but it was still possible for non-elite people to be culturally important – like the Elizabethan dramatist Robert Greene, or the eighteenth-century poet William Hutton. The industrial revolution made it much harder for the working classes to become culturally elite, but the nineteenth century also witnessed attempts by idealistic figures like William Morris to argue that beauty was the preserve of all classes. Then in the early twentieth century there was an extraordinary flourishing of avant-garde art and design that was very explicitly aimed at the poor as well as the rich. There's no reason why those with expertise or artistic judgement should necessarily be well off, therefore, but since the 1970s we have seen the economically privileged pull away from everyone else both in their wealth and in their cultural capital.

I'm not blaming individuals for being posh. The problem is structural. It used to be the case that if you wanted to be an actor, a musician or a journalist, and you needed work experience, you could go on the dole. You could live in a squat. You could get a fully funded university place and do an unpaid internship in the holidays. Now you need support from the Bank of Mum and Dad. Successive governments have removed the sources of funding – social security and block grants – that once enabled those from non-traditional backgrounds to enter elite professions. Writing book reviews used to be a credible job; now it's a hobby. As we've seen, digital mega-corps have thrown young people the bone of 'user as producer' and the lure of free stuff, while closing off realistic entrance routes to actually getting a job in those shimmering creative industries.

Just as elite professions acquire the taint of poshness because of policies that ensure that only the posh are able to enter them, so they acquire the taint of self-serving insularity. The people occupying those roles may themselves be well-heeled, but the industries as a whole are underfunded and shrinking. This is a key distinction. Starved of resources, cultural and media organisations are simply unable to uphold the high standards that the public expect of them.

These two trends, therefore – the narrowing of the social pool from which staff are drawn, and the lack of financial support – means that the quality of the output diminishes more and more: journalists seem ever more complacent, yet they didn't even predict Brexit! The Trumpian denunciation of the mainstream media as 'fake news' is so resonant because it contains within it a grain of truth – the news has become PR-driven, craven and often inaccurate. But this is because of the very undermining of journalism that Trump and his ilk have promoted. The media 'establishment' is presented as bloated and privileged: 'How the liberal media elite failed working-class Americans', ran an illustrative headline in *The Guardian*. Yet the industry itself is on its knees. There is thus a self-perpetuating downward spiral of eroding standards and fading public faith.

The populist right have stripped our political institutions and journalistic and cultural organisations of economic sustenance, reducing them to debased versions of themselves. They then decry them as bastions of elitism and error. Liberals themselves, meanwhile, running scared by these accusations, are unable to defend these vital institutions, because they've forgotten what was valuable about them in the first place. We can all rail at the BBC and at liberal newspapers, calling them corrupt, biased and inaccurate. And then we will look up from our rants and look around for them and Oh! They'll be gone.

Nine

High Art for All

SINCE CLASS AND status have now become equated with education rather than wealth, Trump and other postmodern demagogues can claim the super-rich and the poor alike as their constituency. This conceals the fact that their substantive interests are diametrically opposed. And it also conceals a rich history of working-class intellectualism and cultural activity that has been erased – likewise – by our blind faith in the illusion that cultural 'democratisation' is a novel development.

When a public consultation was launched into the future of the BBC licence fee (the Conservative government disingenuously leaving it up to 'the people' to vote down public support for public service broadcasting), one tweet summed up the prevalent view that high arts and low social status don't go together. 'Oh yes. Ordinary working class folks really do love those orchestras [sceptical face emoji] The BBC need to do more to appeal to the working class folk, and then they can also do the high brow stuff,' they wrote. 'Keep going the way they are and disaster looms.'

This kind of attitude reveals that, in fact, cultural democratisation is itself a sham. By contrast, myriad examples of genuine blue-collar engagement with arts and ideas lie buried in the past. The late nineteenth century saw the emergence of individual and collective proletarian efforts to achieve the best education and experience the highest culture: to read the classics, go to the theatre and listen to classical music. Workers set up mutual improvement societies, cooperative societies and mechanics' institutes. The first working men's club was set up in 1862, and soon there were gasfitters', brassworkers', railwaymen's, miners' and coachmakers' clubs, designed as places for workers – men only, admittedly – to meet for 'conversation, business and mental improvement, with the means of recreation and refreshment'; they boasted libraries and offered a range of courses. The socialist *Clarion* magazine was founded in the 1890s with the aim of reaching a broad readership; it published writing by George Bernard Shaw and artwork by Walter Crane. It was associated with the Workers' Travel Association and a panoply of cycling and rambling clubs, of which the National Clarion Cycling Club still survives. Ruskin Hall, later Ruskin College, was established in 1899 to provide educational opportunities to working people who were denied access to university. It was deliberately placed in Oxford, the home of elite education.

The Workers' Educational Association was founded in 1903; the social historian R. H. Tawney taught the first tutorial classes in Rochdale. Literary and scientific institutes were founded up and down the country, from Essex to Edinburgh, Cardiff to Carlisle. The cultural institutes set up by miners in South Wales were particularly impressive, with reading rooms equipped with a range of daily newspapers, well-stocked libraries, concert halls, ballrooms and rehearsal rooms. Miners read widely – *Das Kapital* but also *Jane Eyre*. By the

Second World War, the Tredegar Workmen's Institute had a library that circulated 100,000 volumes per year, a cinema that could seat 800, regular concerts and a film society.

In *The Intellectual Life of the British Working Classes*, the historian Jonathan Rose uncovers through unpublished diaries and memoirs a lost world of auto-didacticism and informal education. There was the Edwardian housemaid who devoured *Tess of the D'Urbervilles*; the Labour MP Will Crooks, who, growing up in extreme poverty in east London, was dazzled by a second-hand copy of *The Iliad* he bought for 2d; and the Southampton charwoman who read the complete works of Shakespeare on her deathbed. A Nottingham hosiery worker, recalling his childhood at the start of the twentieth century, wrote: 'We loved nothing so much when I was a kid as going to my auntie's and listening to her records – the *Messiah*, the "Triumphal March" from *Aïda*, *Il trovatore*. And a lot of people read Shaw, the pamphlets and the plays, Robert Blatchford, H. G. Wells, Dickens, Thackeray.' Rose tells the story of Jim Turnbull, a self-taught blacksmith in Jarrow, whose library included Chesterton, Belloc, Darwin and a collection of classical records. He bought his nephew Bacon's *Essays* at a 3d bookstall, took him to his first opera (*La bohème*) and showed him the architectural wonders of Newcastle's St Nicholas's Cathedral. 'You'll see the time, son,' he told him, 'when the symphonies of Beethoven and the operas of Mozart will be played in public halls everywhere.'

One of the foremost proponents of high culture for all was William Morris. For Morris, beauty was not anathema to manual labour: good work was bound up with aesthetics and the elevation of the mind. Morris fought the narrow utilitarianism of Jeremy Bentham – for Morris, utility and beauty must be intertwined. In his 1884 lecture 'Art and Socialism', Morris declared that he lived under a system that 'has trampled down Art, and exalted Commerce into a sacred religion'. The result, he went on, was that 'the greater part of the people have no share in Art – which as things now are must be kept in the hands of a few rich or well-to-do people, who we may fairly say need it less and not more than the laborious workers'.

Morris set out to change all that. He became one of a series of thinkers and campaigners who worked to bring culture and education to the masses. There were Beatrice and Sidney Webb, socialist philanthropists who helped found the Fabian Society, and the poet, free-thinker and sexual rebel Edward Carpenter, who moved to Leeds as part of the University Extension Movement, pioneered by academics who wanted to bring higher education to working-class communities in deprived areas of the country. Oscar Wilde was also a passionate advocate of great art and difficult ideas for all. In his 1891 essay 'The Soul of Man under Socialism', he complained that the public 'has always, and in every age, been badly brought up. They are continually asking Art to be popular, to please their want of taste, to flatter their absurd vanity, to tell them what they have been told before.' Art, he continued, 'should never try to be popular. The public should try to make itself artistic.' I'm not denying that these figures could sometimes come across as high-handed or hypocritical, but at least they expressed ideals and opened up debates that are now completely unthinkable.

This nineteenth-century tradition of universal art and education would extend into the twentieth century with the great idealist upsurge of brutalist municipal and council house architecture, and avant-garde theatre. Glasgow's Citizens Theatre combined ambitious repertoire with cheap tickets, free previews and free programmes for every member of the audience. Public bodies such as the British Academy and the Open University expressed the widespread ethos that the arts and humanities were a public good in and of themselves. Public service broadcasting beamed the work of television auteurs into ordinary living rooms around the country, including Dennis Potter's *Pennies from Heaven* and *The Singing Detective*. BBC1's *Wednesday Play* and its successor, *Play for Today*, broadcast between 1964 and 1984, featured innovative, on-location dramas by Mike Leigh, Alan Clarke, Stephen Frears, Ken Loach and Stephen Poliakoff: sometimes, it should be said, in the teeth of objections from BBC executives. *Cathy Come Home*, Loach's realist drama about homelessness, attracted 12 million viewers, a quarter of the British population at the time. ITV launched *The South*

Bank Show in 1978; Channel 4 screened arthouse films late into the night. It was the era of what the late cultural theorist Mark Fisher called the age of 'popular modernism', enabled by the post-1945 settlement with its generous welfare provision and university grants for working-class art school students. As Fisher wrote:

> In a seeming irony, the media class's refusal to be paternalistic has not produced a bottom-up culture of breath-taking diversity, but one that is increasingly infantilized. By contrast, it is paternalistic cultures that treat audiences as adults, assuming that they can cope with cultural products that are complex and intellectually demanding.

The rot set in from the 1980s onwards, as Margaret Thatcher dismantled the welfare state and the public began to automatically associate popular demand with the commercial imperative. This shift was not the result, as is commonly stated, of the expansion of higher education. As Raymond Williams argued in his 1958 essay 'Culture is Ordinary', mass education did not lead to

bad mass culture. Nor is it the case that the highest
criticism always concerned itself with the highest culture. Figures like Clive James, and publications like the
Modern Review, were intelligent takes on popular culture – TV soaps, mainstream pop, even adverts. Just as
it's still possible to point to some great shows, it is not
that this kind of cultural criticism doesn't go on any
more – *The Wire* and The Quietus are good contemporary examples – but it's now on the fringes. Clive
James's reviews of Pinter plays and *Dallas* alike; the
BBC's *The Late Show* and *Late Review* – all were once
water-cooler fare. Now we just fetishise the arts and
crafts aesthetic and mid-century brutalism: there are
tea towels emblazoned with the Barbican building, and
even a corduroy-wearing, banjo-playing band called –
and I share their nostalgia – Public Service Broadcasting.

Back in 1965, Lyndon Johnson's Arts and Humanities Bill declared: 'The arts and the humanities belong to
all the people of the United States', people of 'all backgrounds', wherever they are located. The job of federal
government, it stated, was to 'transmit the achievement
and values of civilization from the past via the present

to the future, and make widely available the greatest achievement of art'. 'We will create a National Theater to bring ancient and modern classics of the theater to audiences all over America,' Johnson said in his speech to mark the bill's signing. 'We will support a National Opera Company and a National Ballet Company. We will create an American Film Institute, bringing together leading artists of the film industry, outstanding educators, and young men and women who wish to pursue the twentieth-century art form as their life's work.' These programmes would serve 'not only the needs of the body and the demands of commerce but the desire for beauty and the hunger for community'. We would do well to remember such ambition.

Ten

'Deference Is Dead'

I F WE AS a society are to uphold beauty and truth
on their own terms, as neither the playthings of
the privileged nor the instrumental tools of social
mobility – a lofty aim I know, but essential nonetheless – we need to be able to say what these qualities are.
But, as Rónán McDonald argues in *The Death of the
Critic*, the old umpires have been given their march-
ing orders by those who unfairly associate them with
elevated social status. Criticism – defined as discernment, applying informed judgement, ranking one thing
higher than something else and explaining why – has
been replaced by fandom. Fandom is not always uncrit-
ical, and it's often very knowledgeable – but it offers
minute detail rather than stepping-back perspective.

Hot takes are necessarily unconsidered. Internet memes offer riffs, not purchase.

We're knocking the cultural gatekeepers off their plinths, imposing a soft Maoist revolution in our universities, and laying waste to the up-itself political establishment. We now trust the great British public. But there's a snag. Take TripAdvisor. It's the poster boy for the hive mind. Yet it's unfailingly useless as a way of choosing a place to visit or stay or grab a bite to eat that's actually good, rather than just somewhere that's corporate and bland and where the managers have avoided run-ins with guests by being glassily professional and anodyne. The Blue Guides and Michelin Green Guides may be austerely hard to please, but at least their view is trustworthy. Or take Airbnb, a great way to find a cheap apartment or rent out your spare room if you're a member of the creative precariat; but if your guests trash your flat, there's no adult in the room, no authority you can turn to who'll sort it out. Everyone just gives everyone else five stars out of politeness – or no stars if they've had a personal disagreement. Wikipedia, held as proof of the wisdom of the crowd, is very accurate, but that's because it references published scholarship; it's also worth saying that 77 per cent of its content has been written by just 1 per cent of its (mostly white, Western, male) editors.

This mass iconoclasm has left us all with a problem – not just snobs like me, but everyone. We still desperately need sources of validation and arbiters of quality. This paradox is clear to anyone who watches *The Great British Bake Off*. Yes, the show features 'ordinary' people. But everyone hangs reverently on the decisions of the judges, and especially those of Prue Leith, the primary expert in the room. The same is true of Simon Cowell on *The X Factor* and *Britain's Got Talent*. These people are valued because they have expertise rather than just an opinion, and dare to say what they think.

While 'gatekeepers' are now routinely denigrated as defenders of entitlement, they are simultaneously worshipped in a disavowed way that enables us to avoid facing head-on the incoherence of the situation. Aspiring musicians extol the instantaneity of YouTube but regard as a marker of true success a contract with an established record company and coverage in the NME.

In this transitional moment where old and new forms of distribution and validation coexist, traditional media cravenly applauds the advent of the platforms that will result in their demise, while viral new-media success stories are a *thing* only because old media still exists to report them. My students are glued to their phones but also attached to old models of achievement, like becoming magazine journalists or radio presenters, regardless of the fact that their precious internet is eroding the possibility of that success. And who can blame them? We are all addicts now. Just as our culture venerates as never before cultural, creative and media jobs, and encourages ever greater numbers of students to go to university to do Media Studies, the digital 'revolution' – hailed as so empowering – is, in lockstep with global capitalism, eviscerating cultural and journalistic industries and radically reducing the number of openings, which intensifies competition yet further.

The exponential rise of Creative Writing encapsulates these tensions. While I teach the discipline myself and I do believe that studying it is worthwhile, particularly the emphasis on writing as a tangible craft, it does channel some problematic cultural trends. There's a danger that our logical destination as a society is a dubious utopia in which the number of writers will far exceed the number of books professionally published; and all professional writers will have to teach Creative Writing to get by. Audience becomes author, but this will not constitute a level playing field. Even those who make an enthusiastic case for self-publishing and self-publicity via social media cling to existing modes of evaluation. Fan fiction, the subject of a great deal of contemporary scholarly excitement, purports to blur the distinction between author and reader. But it relies on a downplayed power differential between admired and admirer, original and pastiche. The proliferating writing courses advertised in broadsheets are a contingent life-form, feeding off a temporary gradient between professional and aspiring writers.

Still attached as we are to traditional sources of affirmation, we have displaced our need for critical judgement and evaluation onto numbers of likes and followers, ratings systems and starred reviews. We rejoice at getting rid of the hierarchy of judgement, but this has simply been replaced by an even more sharp-elbowed yet less overt hierarchy of hive-mind limelight-jostling and algorithmic ranking. These systems appear to be spontaneous and vernacular, crucially different from something as top-down and old-school as bureaucracy, but they are simply a different – and more pernicious – form of audit.

The well-publicised fantasy of any reasonably talented individual being able to become a recording artist or a political commentator by showcasing their work online is undermined by the fact that we only have limited attention for strangers' raps on YouTube or their polemics on Twitter – and in practice there's the same monopoly of public attention as there was in the old, real world. In fact, it's even worse, because at least in the past there was a healthy ecosystem of newspapers and publishers, and middle-rung commentators and authors could get a certain amount of exposure. Now we have a handful of superstars and everyone else grubbing around for crumbs. The new model is the same old dominators plus a noisily advertised sprinkling of grassroots or BAME 'new voices'. Instead of Kenneth Clark's patrician lectures in *Civilisation*, the landmark 1969 BBC series on Western art and culture, we've had the new, diversely presented *Civilisations* plural, but the white male Simon Schama still played the most prominent role. The point about the old lectures was that they were authored and therefore told from an explicitly particular viewpoint. Now our presenters purport to be 'everyman' – Antony Gormley's facile figures come to mind as an artistic parallel – they 'tell stories' and undergo immersive experiences – the critical element is gone.

The breakdown of our systems of recognition and approval obscures the persistence, even strengthening, of the most iniquitous forms of power and privilege. The old guard have simply been replaced with new, more informal authorities and celebrities dangling unrealistic prospects of accessible kudos. White, male, private school-educated TV executives opine on festival platforms about how the old era of white, male presenters 'mansplaining on hilltops' is definitively over; yet television is dominated more than ever by those very same mansplainers – just now with an outsiderish, maverick veneer.

Eleven

A New Defence of
Good Elitism

A S A CULTURE, we have collectively thrown up our hands and declared that we can't possibly define aesthetic value; to do so would be impossibly elitist. Anyone who presumes to seriously appreciate or critique art must be privileged and wealthy, we tell ourselves, and therefore themselves elite. Yet during the eighteenth century, the question of what makes something beautiful was the subject of lively public debate. Philosophers, poets and writers grabbed with both hands the task of defining beauty – and truth, for that matter – and their conclusions were picked over by a surprisingly engaged public.

Ancient philosophers including Plato, Aristotle and Saint Augustine had kicked off the discussion, arguing that beauty was an objective quality, intrinsic to the artwork itself. But speed along to the seventeenth century and John Locke challenged this, arguing that beauty was a matter of subjective perception and appreciation – it was in the eye of the beholder. Subsequent philosophers took a middle way: in his 1757 essay 'Of the Standard of Taste', David Hume pointed out that although judgement may be subjective, critics tend to agree on what is good, and classics stand the test of time. In the same year, Edmund Burke published his influential *Philosophical Inquiry into the Origin of Our Ideas of the Sublime and Beautiful*, which asserted that although beauty is about perception via the senses, those responses can still be sorted into categories. Immanuel Kant's *Critique of Judgement*, published in 1790, took an even more rationalistic approach to analysing how we appreciate beauty. These now-unfashionable questions weren't necessarily answered definitively, but there was at least an attempt to grapple with them. And, more than this, the figure of the critic was robustly defended

– in Alexander Pope's *Essay on Criticism*, and in the writer-politician Joseph Addison's positive portrayal of the critic as 'arbiter of taste'.

The rise of Enlightenment reason, and its rigorous attempts to engage with these questions of beauty and perception, was a response to the airy assumptions and privileged monopoly of the Tory church-and-crown establishment. The progressive notion that aesthetic value could be argued over and worked out in public was embodied in political and literary magazines like Samuel Johnson's *Rambler*, the thrice-weekly *Tatler*, founded by another writer-politician, Richard Steele, and *The Spectator*, set up in 1711 by Steele and Addison, in an attempt to bring these definitions to thousands of modest households. Their aim was to bring philosophy 'out of closets and libraries, schools, and colleges, to dwell in clubs and assemblies, at tea-tables and in coffee-houses'. This puts a different spin on our contemporary notion of a metropolitan elite: this was a decidedly urban and intellectual culture, but one that was also an inclusive and sceptical challenge to the landowning class.

This tradition of defining, critiquing and validating

the arts carried on into the nineteenth century. In his 1864 essay 'The Function of Criticism at the Present Time', Matthew Arnold argued that the arts flourish in the context of criticism – this is in contrast to the modern idea that criticism is an enemy of the arts. True culture, he wrote, 'does not try to teach down to the level of inferior classes' but rather 'seeks to do away with classes; to make the best that has been thought and known in the world current everywhere; to make all men live in an atmosphere of sweetness and light, where they may use ideas … freely – nourished, and not bound by them'. And then in the twentieth century, from F. R. Leavis to Northrop Frye, I. A. Richards to William Empson, a whole generation of literary critics wrestled with these questions of quality and what should be included in the canon, the collectively agreed list – in Arnold's terms – of 'the best that has been thought and known in the world'.

That aim has been undermined in our own time by the realisation that the 'canon' has been made up predominantly of white men. This is true but for historical and circumstantial reasons and is therefore not a justification to dispense with the idea of quality altogether. As

Jonathan Rose showed, working-class readers favoured the same great classics as the upper classes did. Today, the traditional canon is under attack from two very different sides. The identity politics agenda and the very widespread attempts to 'decolonise' the canon and the curriculum in higher education are very much at odds with the populist agenda of serving 'left-behind' communities, implicitly presumed to be white working class. That constituency is defined in opposition to race- and gender-based identity politics. The answer is surely to look harder for outstanding marginalised voices that have been excluded by the self-reproducing tendencies of canon formation. As we've seen, the other force undermining efforts to bring truly great art to a wider audience is our discomfort with the whole notion that we could judge one thing to be better than another. In his anti-elitist book *What Good Are the Arts?*, John Carey argues that any judgement of aesthetic quality that is not entirely random must be grounded in the divine. I don't agree. Judgements about quality and accuracy are neither a free-for-all nor an absolute but are determined by communities and institutions.

There's another lesson worth taking from the Enlightenment. The proliferation of philosophical debates about aesthetics in the eighteenth century was accompanied by the rise of the professions, embodied in the Royal Societies and other learned associations. These two developments had in common a single principle: that the process of deciding what is beautiful and what is true cannot be taken for granted as obvious but should be deliberately reasoned out. It's important not to uncritically revere these institutions and processes and regard them as infallible. And it's true that those who have made up those learned societies, and those who still do make decisions now, tend once again to be overwhelmingly white, male and privileged. But that's not an argument for getting rid of those thinkers and decision-makers altogether. Because the alternative is not democratisation but either aristocratically imposed standards or no standards at all.

Over centuries, we have built up a complex web of trust relationships based on treatises, articles, reports, accounts and public records. Experts have been employed for the common good. Franklin Roosevelt's

'Brains Trust' planned the New Deal in the 1930s, which rebuilt America after the Great Depression. A group of economists led by John Maynard Keynes met at Bretton Woods after the Second World War, putting in place a system for regulating the banks which has since been undermined, resulting in the Great Recession of 2008–09. It is not that the truth and aesthetic standards were once set in stone and are now being radically questioned. It's that since the seventeenth and eighteenth centuries, we've built up institutional ways of determining these questions. This is not about fixed certainties but about workable arrangements. Authority is about reasoned consensus underpinned by research and evidence.

It is those arrangements that are now breaking down, undermined by the combined forces of digital technology and global capitalism that are in turn legitimated by the widespread illusion that this constitutes people-powered progress. Just as attacks on the mainstream media have led not to vibrant citizen journalism but to PR-handled selective news briefings and Facebook 'People's PMQs', the culture of criticism has been replaced by homogenous consumerism and the commercial imperative, by film and theatre puff pieces and the blanket promotion of fewer and fewer titles by chain bookstores. Rather than empowering readers, the loss of critical authority and the decline of the value placed on knowledgeable judgement has played into the hands of monopolies.

Some believe that the public will never trust experts again; that verification and knowledge will have to be radically redistributed to all via some online platform. I don't think that will work. Not everyone has the time or energy to become an expert or an armchair investigative reporter, and it's not a good idea to leave it to algorithms. Such revolutionary proposals are in any case a big distraction from the real, economic abuses of power. In her 2019 report into future funding models for high-quality journalism, Frances Cairncross pointed out that sometimes the job of challenging such abuses has to be imposed top-down. 'The stories people want to read may not always be the ones that they ought to read in order to ensure that a democracy can hold its public servants properly to account,' she said. There's a fine line between the 'grassroots' and market forces.

Professionalisation is a double-edged sword. It can be a negative quality, as in the professionalised politician – and it can refer to the cultivation and protection of opaque received assumptions. But it can also mean professionalism: the development of agreed standards for judgements and actions. Professions – like political institutions – need to be able to act in private some of the time: relentless demands for continuous transparency divert resources from the real work and undermine the capacity for considered decision-making. A successful democracy relies on established norms and traditions, institutional checks and balances, and careful deliberation behind closed doors – all of which can appear shady and aloof. Unless we defend and reframe these principles for a post-deferential age, the anti-system right will continue to undermine the only structures and mechanisms we have for enacting large-scale change.

In the populist era, complaints about corruption are commonplace (they've all got their snouts in the same trough); yet financial motives seem more transparent than the closed worlds of political protocol and professional knowledge. By flashing his cash (literally being photographed boarding Air Force One with $20 bills hanging out his back pocket), Trump signals to his supporters that he has nothing to hide, unlike Capitol Hill insiders; all politicians lie, he implies with his outrageous tweets, but at least he does so openly.

Right now, it's officials and organisations that aim, at least in principle, to look after and serve the public that are the targets of aggressive demands for disclosure – from the diplomats embarrassed by WikiLeaks to MPs' expenses to the Leveson inquiry into phone hacking (which rightly exposed abuses but added another nail to the coffin of the fourth estate). It's tempting to take down politicians, journalists and state bodies because they are already in a defensive crouch. The combination of their vulnerability and their slightly desperate projection of moral authority provides those precious gotcha moments we all thirst after in a maddeningly disempowered age. Just as voting Leave induced a temporary thrill, taking down the apparent elites is a simulacrum for netting the real elites. It's not as if big finance lacks its own secrets and lies – take the rigging of Libor as a single example – but they seem just too powerful and elusive to nail.

We treat public institutions as if they are a mother that has failed to look after us. The 'dads' are business and finance, striding around out of sight, taking risks and creating jobs. MPs on right and left alike dismiss the 'nanny' state as a condescending relic of the past century. But the principle of a social safety net simply acknowledges that, at certain points throughout our lives, we humans need looking after. In her 1954 essay 'The Crisis in Education', Hannah Arendt argued that authority did not involve looking down on people; it indicated that someone was taking responsibility. But now, more and more people are swallowing the lie that politicians, experts, professionals and journalists are on the wrong side of a culture war. Authority, institutions – these are the most unfunky, unfashionable concepts around; but we junk them at our peril.

Here we come back to the baby and the bathwater. The public distrusts the expert 'establishment' because they think they are in cahoots and marking each other's homework. This gives licence to the populists to burn the whole thing down. But what if our standards and systems of scrutiny themselves were improved? What if they were made not more transparent, necessarily, but more rigorous? The more we distrust and attack experts, the more energy they pour into performing conscientious accountability rather than simply going about their business with integrity. But we could do much to raise professional standards. We could make peer review less comfortable and cosy. We could make qualifications and grades meaningful rather than a slap on the back or a tick in a box. Expert judgement could be implemented according to democratic processes: after all, decision-making is not neutral; it's up for grabs and open to debate. These decisions are human and they are in our hands. We have the power to defend what we decide we positively value. We don't have to leave those decisions to the impersonal forces of markets or machines.

At a time when nobody is standing up for what is wise and beautiful in our culture, and the positive conception of authority that goes with it, it's time for us to start to talk once again about what high standards look like. I do not have the answers, but I propose we once again start asking the questions. In an age of popular hostility to the old establishment, we need to have an inclusive conversation about how these standards can be developed collectively and fairly: not based on blind traditions of connoisseurship but derived from reasoned judgement, deliberation, knowledge and experience. At a time when democracy and civilisation are being destroyed for the benefit of the real power elite, all in the name of 'the people', we need to come together to invent new institutions, standards and forms of authority that aren't associated with the crumbling dinosaur models and privileged discernments of the past. Otherwise, disparities of wealth will become ever sharper, while our cultural and intellectual lives will dissolve into mediocrity. In our cowed concession to populist snake oil merchants, we are forgetting the old aim of placing the pursuit of knowledge above that of profit.

Politicians, we are told, are out of touch. Broadsheet commentators should have spent more time in Scunthorpe and Nuneaton if they wanted to understand the concerns of 'ordinary' people. Maybe we should get out there and start listening? The injunction to 'listen' contains – once again – a grain of truth. Cosmopolitan progressives – those whom Piketty calls the 'Brahmin left' – do need to work once again to forge alliances with those who are culturally and educationally very different to them. Technocratic Third Way politicians like Blair and Clinton advocated policy derived from 'what works' as a way of concealing their ideological agenda. Their claim to be 'beyond ideology' has in common with the instruction to 'listen' a counterproductive reluctance to state what one's political beliefs and diagnoses really are. When people advocate 'listening' in that angry way, they speak almost as if the consequences of austerity and the dismantling of the welfare state aren't grossly apparent all around us: in the queues outside citizens' advice bureaus, and in the ranks of the homeless lying like rubbish in the street.

We need to listen, but we need to also start saying uncomfortable things, too. It's time for progressives to free themselves from the muddle they have got into about 'elitism'; to stop feeling petrified of being branded culpably highbrow or bubble-bound if they stand up for what they believe is true and important. It's time to bring together the values of egalitarianism and intellectualism.

It's time to defend professional expertise, high culture, political representation and well-resourced journalistic scrutiny. It's time for a progressive defence of good elitism.

The shift we need is about practicalities as well as principles; it's about, for example, new ways of enabling high culture to be produced. The universal basic income is the go-to panacea for many exhausted utopians, but it makes sense for creatives and those working in disappearing media industries. There is no good reason not to bring back block grants for students and boost state funding for the arts. We could find a new funding model for journalism that actually works, or just buy and fund newspapers – the only model that has worked so far. We could rein back bureaucracy in public institutions and sweep away the empty and implacable demands on public bodies to be 'accountable to the public purse'. We could trust professionals, academics and artists to get on with what they want to do, rather than making them waste time on inefficient performances of public value – all those grant-bidding and form-filling and 'quality and standards' rituals. We could reinstate intellectual, meaningful standards in universities so students have something to aspire to and work towards.

The right were once the upholders of authority and high-mindedness in politics and the arts alike. But they have now become anti-system populists, scorched-earth reformers and barbaric green-belt developers. Whenever anyone now objects to cutting spending on the arts, or to concreting the countryside, they are liable to be denounced as snobs. Meanwhile, progressives have forgotten valuable historic traditions of radical aestheticism and become timid and tongue-tied, stricken to silence in the face of anti-elitist attacks. While Conservatives have become merciless modernisers, promoting a virulent compound of economic elitism and cultural populism, the left are failing utterly to make the case for positive forms of authority and high standards. Why should the right have a monopoly on the best human civilisation has to offer? Why should Boris Johnson be able to spout Latin aphorisms while the rest of us read pap?

We must not let right-wing populists use culture to undermine vital political action. Redressing inequality should be the job of politics. Cultural excellence

should be disentangled from social privilege. The best
art and ideas should available to everyone, not just the
wealthy. Culture is more than entertainment: it makes us
reflect, it stretches us; it lifts us away from the immediate
and the everyday. When asked about the charge that his
poems are 'difficult', the poet Geoffrey Hill responded,
'Human beings are difficult. We're difficult to ourselves,
we're difficult to each other.' He continued, 'Why is it
believed that poetry, prose, painting, music should be
less than we are?' It is genuinely difficult art, he con-
cluded, that is truly democratic.

We must also protect culture because to do so is a
political act. Culture that exists in its own right is an
inherent riposte to the utilitarian overwork ethos that
has taken over our lives. And art is also politically challenging. Rather than simply being a source of pleasure
and diversion, novels symbolised radicalism and revolution to Victorian factory workers, 'not just because
they preached the right kind of left politics', Jonathan
Rose writes, 'but because they allowed working people
to control their own minds'. The same is true today. Culture should not be the continuation of politics through

other means, therefore, but culture is political. And that's because quality of life, which includes the appreciation of beauty, and quality of place, which involves the protection of nature, should be pursued as the highest political ideals. In her book *The Fight for Beauty*, Fiona Reynolds reminds us that politicians once cited the aesthetic aspect of the countryside as an argument for its protection. Yet now arguments are solely made on the grounds of spurious utility and economic growth. Saving the countryside is represented as elitist by multimillionaire property developers who'd prefer to ignore those plentiful but more awkward brownfield sites: you mean you don't want to help solve the housing crisis?

In the distant or not-too-distant future, when demagoguery has become thoroughly normalised, when BBC broadcasting is a nostalgic memory and the victory by Lady Hale with her spider brooch over the prorogation of Parliament is dimly remembered as the rule of law's last gasp, we will ask ourselves how we let this happen. How could we have handed over power and control, so easily and without a fight, to the oligarchs and populist liars? The explanation lies in anti-elitism.

We are persuading ourselves that we are finally levelling the playing fields between an establishment who – no matter how far they are humbled – are still called complacent and those left-behind communities who – no matter how much we continue to neglect them materially – are still claimed to possess the only authentic voice. Let's overturn this damaging delusion while we still have something to save.